mini

FOR ORGANS, PIANOS & ELECTRONIC KEYBOARDS

E-Z PLAY TODAY

3

ISBN 978-1-4950-7720-3

HAL•LEONARD®

7777 W. BLUEMOUND RD. P.O. BOX 13819 MILWAUKEE, WI 53213

E-Z Play® Today Music Notation © 1975 by HAL LEONARD LLC
E-Z PLAY and EASY ELECTRONIC KEYBOARD MUSIC are registered trademarks of HAL LEONARD LLC.

Visit Hal Leonard Online at
www.halleonard.com

100 KIDS' SONGS

A-Tisket A-Tasket

Registration 9
Rhythm: Fox Trot or Swing

Traditional

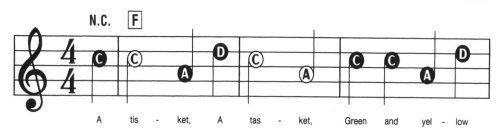

A tis - ket, A tas - ket, Green and yel - low

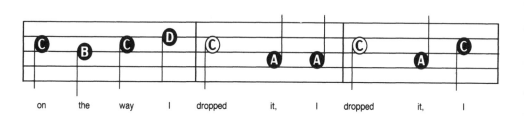

bas - ket, I wrote a let - ter to my love and

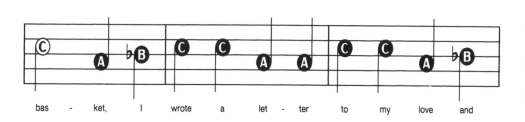

on the way I dropped it, I dropped it, I

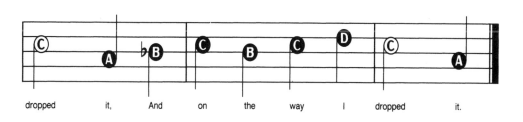

dropped it, And on the way I dropped it.

A-Hunting We Will Go

Registration 4
Rhythm: 6/8 March

Traditional

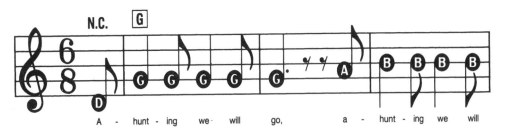

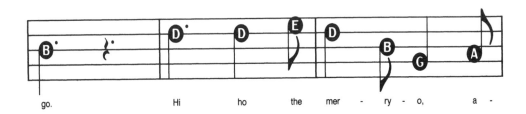

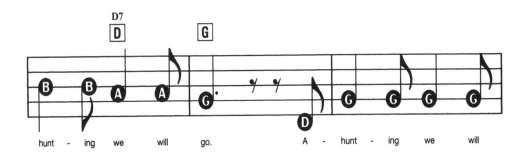

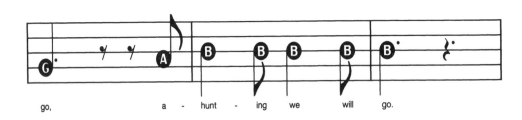

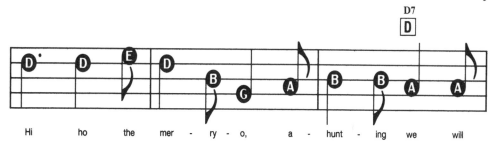

Hi ho the mer - ry - o, a - hunt - ing we will

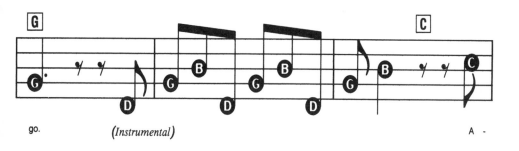

go.   (Instrumental)   A -

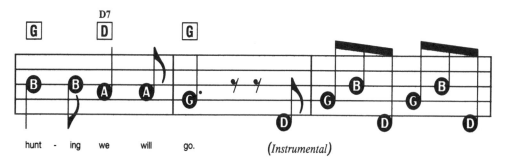

hunt - ing we will go.   (Instrumental)

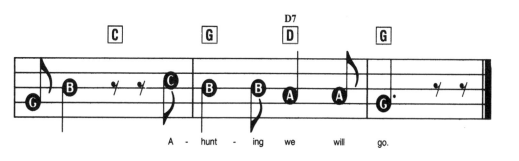

A - hunt - ing we will go.

All Night, All Day

Registration 2
Rhythm: Gospel or Fox Trot

Spiritual

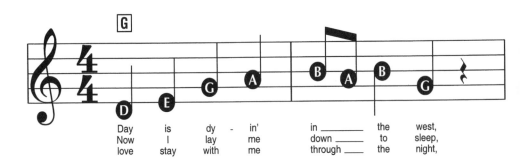

Day   is   dy - in'   in _____ the   west,
Now   I   lay   me   down _____ to   sleep,
love   stay   with   me   through ___ the   night,

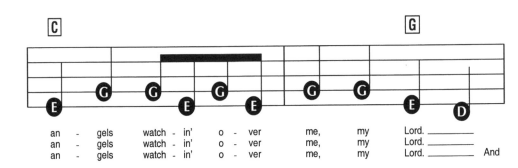

an - gels   watch - in'   o - ver   me,   my   Lord. _____
an - gels   watch - in'   o - ver   me,   my   Lord. _____
an - gels   watch - in'   o - ver   me,   my   Lord. _____ And

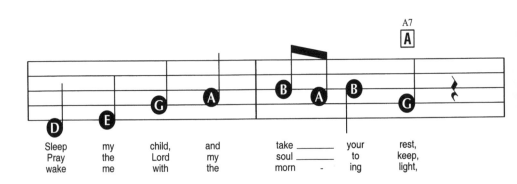

Sleep   my   child,   and   take _____ your   rest,
Pray   the   Lord   my   soul _____ to   keep,
wake   me   with   the   morn - ing   light,

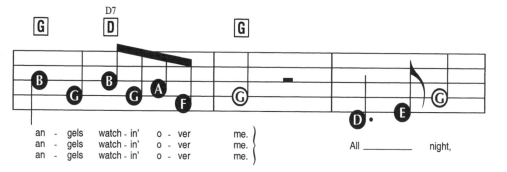

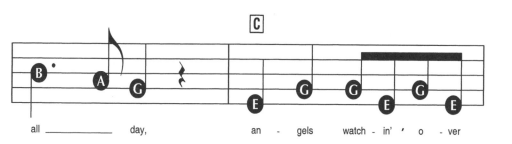

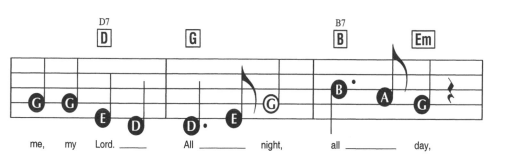

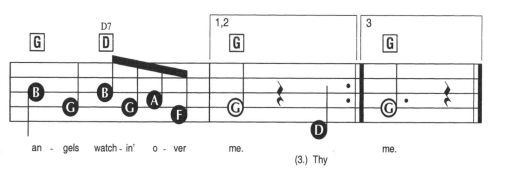

8

Alouette

Registration 3
Rhythm: Fox Trot or Swing

Traditional

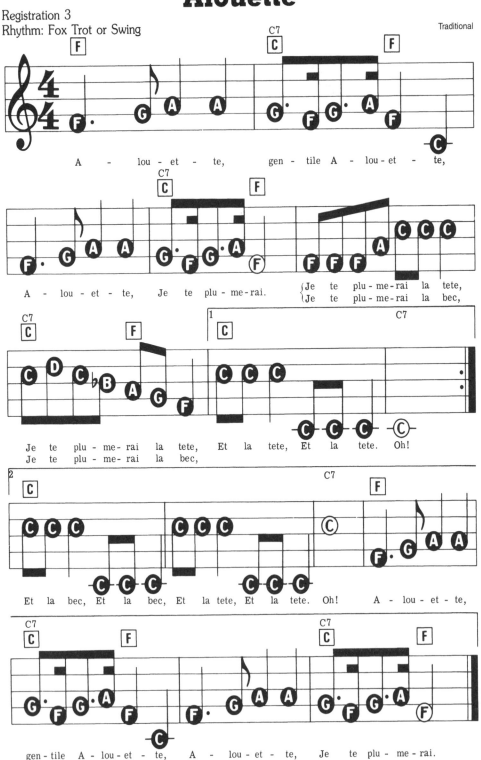

A - lou - et - te, gen - tile A - lou - et - te,

A - lou - et - te, Je te plu - me - rai.

{ Je te plu - me - rai la tete,
{ Je te plu - me - rai la bec,

Je te plu - me - rai la tete, Et la tete, Et la tete. Oh!
Je te plu - me - rai la bec,

Et la bec, Et la bec, Et la tete, Et la tete. Oh! A - lou - et - te,

gen - tile A - lou - et - te, A - lou - et - te, Je te plu - me - rai.

Alphabet Song

Registration 8
Rhythm: Fox Trot

Traditional

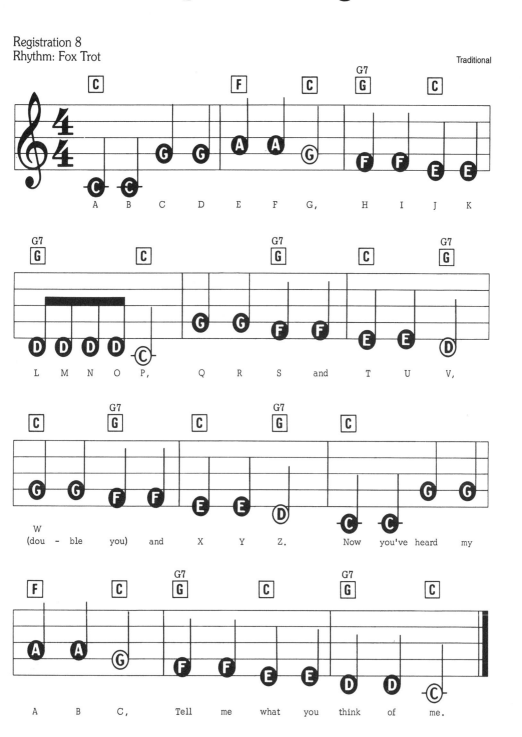

America the Beautiful

Registration 3
Rhythm: March or Fox Trot

Words by Katherine Lee Bates
Music by Samuel A. Ward

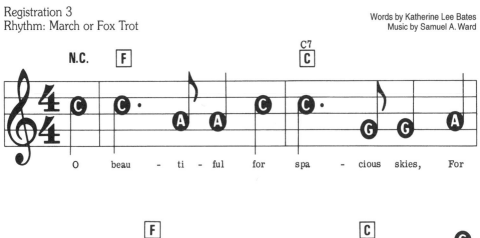

O beau - ti - ful for spa - cious skies, For

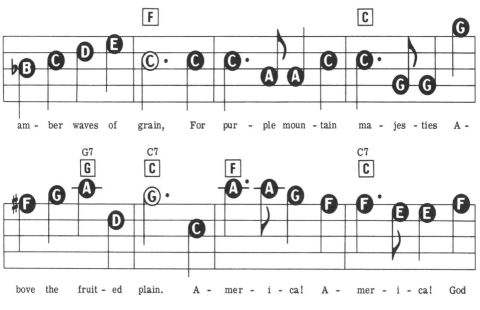

am - ber waves of grain, For pur - ple moun - tain ma - jes - ties A -

bove the fruit - ed plain. A - mer - i - ca! A - mer - i - ca! God

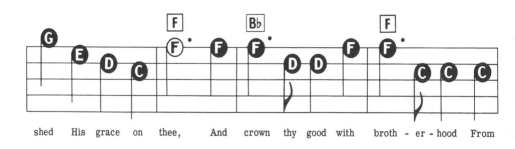

shed His grace on thee, And crown thy good with broth - er - hood From

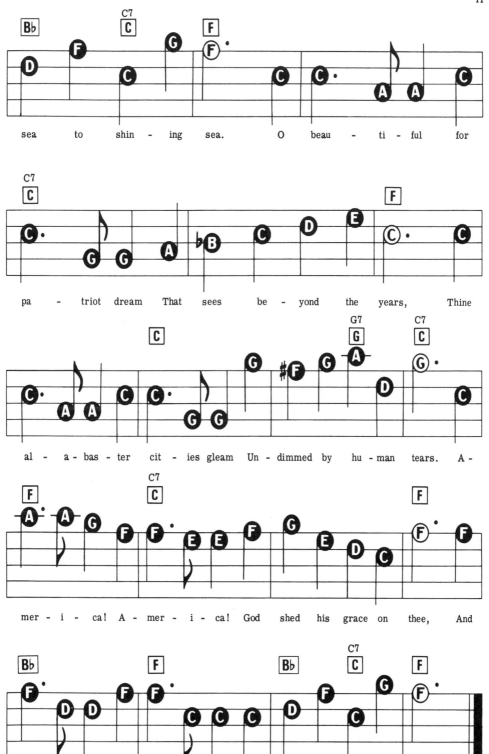

Animal Fair

Registration 4
Rhythm: 6/8 March

American Folksong

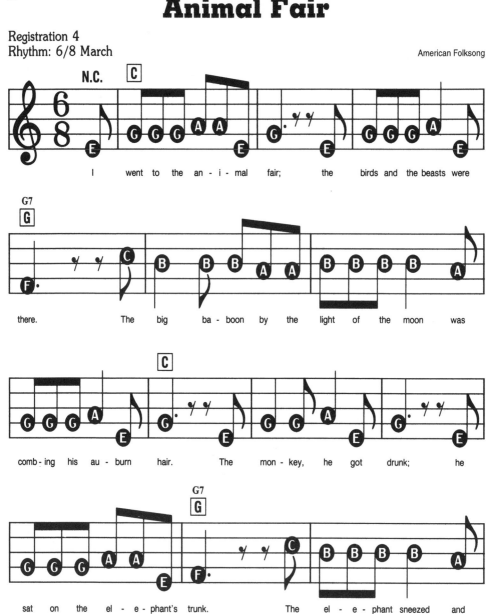

I went to the an - i - mal fair; the birds and the beasts were there. The big ba - boon by the light of the moon was comb - ing his au - burn hair. The mon - key, he got drunk; he sat on the el - e - phant's trunk. The el - e - phant sneezed and

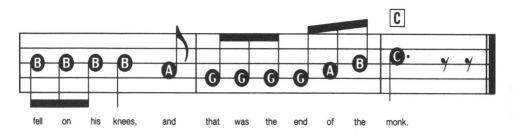

fell on his knees, and that was the end of the monk.

Baa Baa Black Sheep

Registration 2
Rhythm: Fox Trot

Traditional

Baa, baa, black sheep have you an – y wool?

Yes, sir, yes, sir, three bags full,

One for my mas – ter, one for my dame, But

none for the lit – tle boy who cries in the lane.

Barnyard Song

Registration 8
Rhythm: Waltz

Traditional

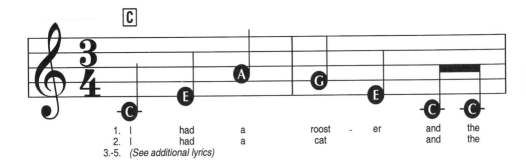

1. I had a roost - er and the
2. I had a cat and the
3.-5. *(See additional lyrics)*

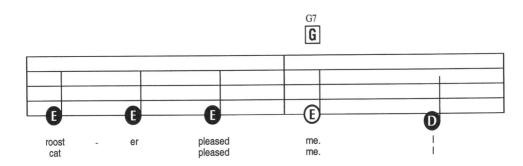

roost - er pleased me.
cat pleased me.

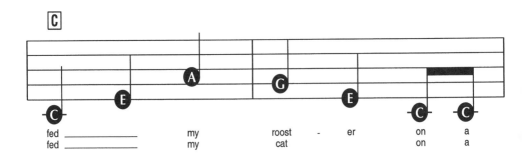

fed _____ my roost - er on a
fed _____ my cat on a

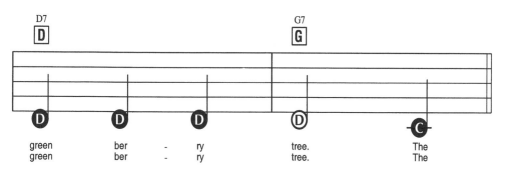

green   ber - ry   tree.   The
green   ber - ry   tree.   The

1st time omit these 4 measures.
For verses 2-5 repeat as needed.

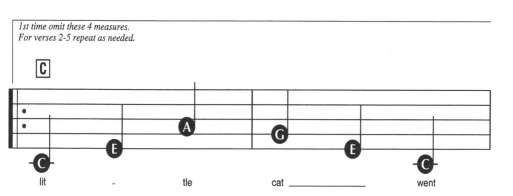

lit - tle   cat _____ went

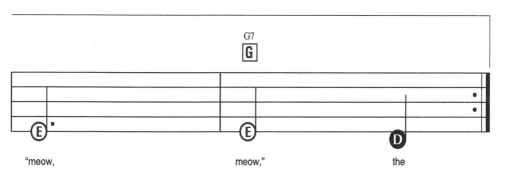

"meow,   meow,"   the

Chorus

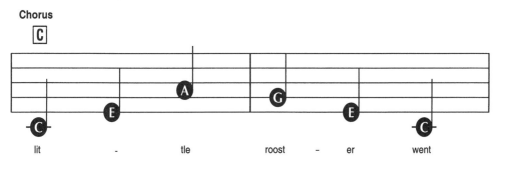

lit - tle   roost - er   went

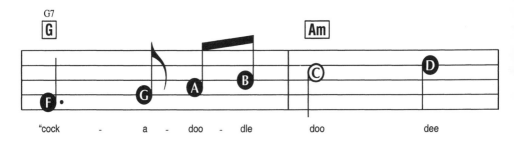

"cock - a - doo - dle doo dee

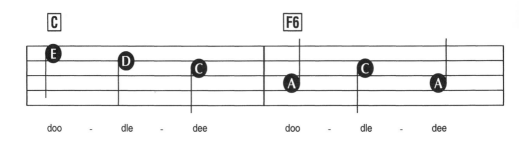

doo - dle - dee doo - dle - dee

D.C.
(Return to beginning
for verses 2-5)

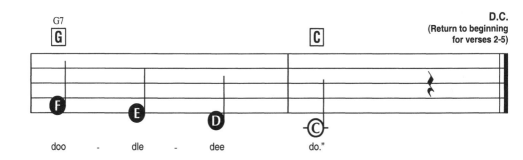

doo - dle - dee do."

Additional Lyrics

3. I had a pig and the pig pleased me.
   I fed my pig on a green berry tree.
   The little pig went "oink oink."
   The little cat went "meow meow."
   Chorus:

4. I had a cow and the cow pleased me.
   I fed my cow on a green berry tree.
   The little cow went "moo moo."
   The little pig went "oink oink."
   The little cat went "meow meow."
   Chorus:

5. I had a baby and the baby pleased me.
   I fed my baby on a green berry tree.
   The little baby went "waah waah."
   The little cow went "moo moo."
   The little pig went "oink oink."
   The little cat went "meow meow."
   Chorus:

Bingo

Registration 8
Rhythm: Fox Trot or Swing

Traditional

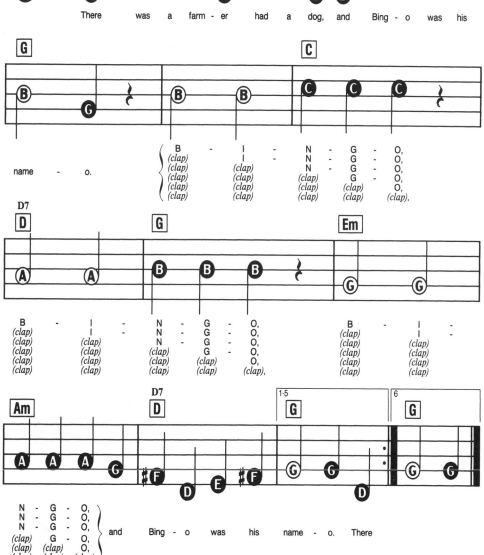

Be Kind to Your
Web-Footed Friends

Registration 5
Rhythm: March or Polka

Traditional

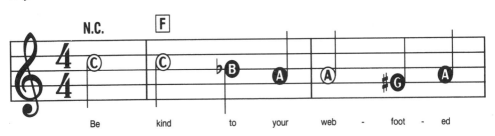

N.C.   F

Be   kind   to   your   web - foot - ed

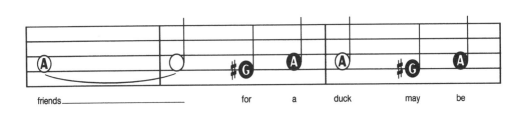

friends_____ for   a   duck   may   be

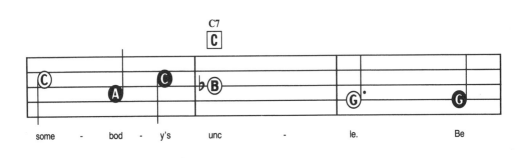

C7
C

some - bod - y's   unc - le.   Be

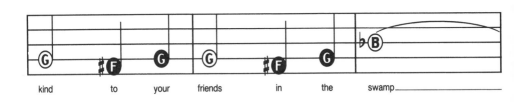

kind   to   your   friends   in   the   swamp_____

19

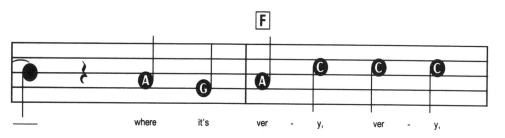

where it's ver - y, ver - y,

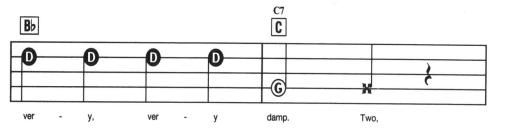

ver - y, ver - y damp. Two,

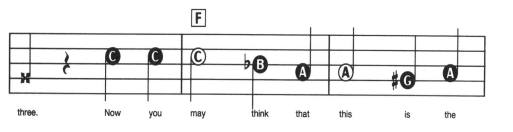

three. Now you may think that this is the

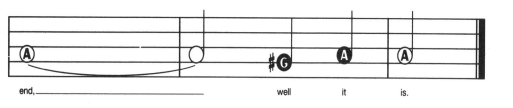

end, well it is.

The Bear Went Over the Mountain

Registration 9
Rhythm: Waltz

Traditional

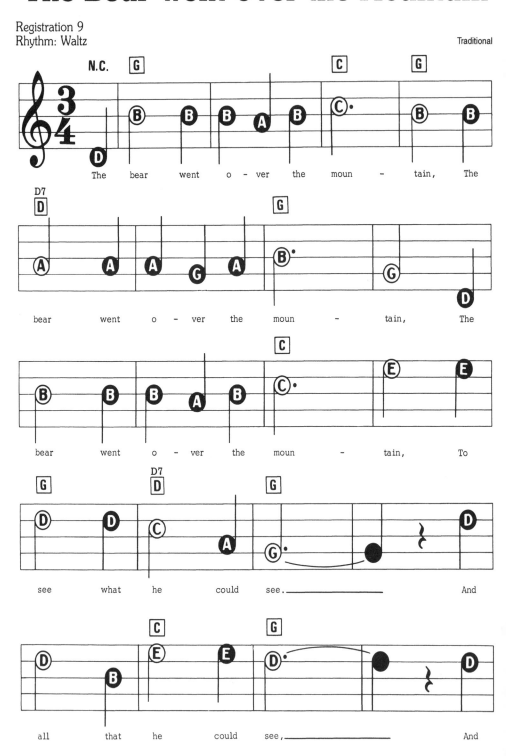

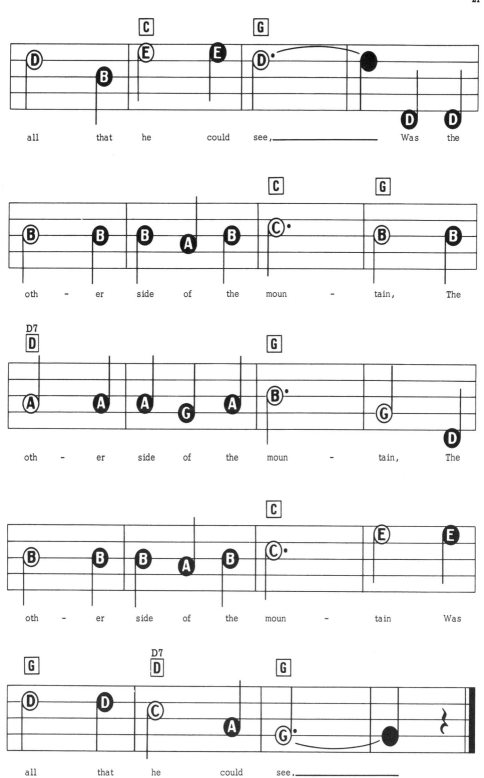

The Blue Tail Fly
(Jimmy Crack Corn)

Registration 4
Rhythm: Fox Trot

Words and Music by
Daniel Decatur Emmett

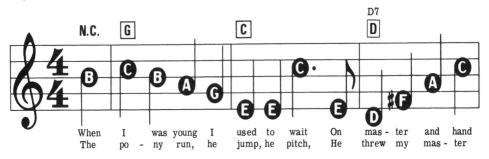

When I was young I used to wait On mas - ter and hand
The po - ny run, he jump, he pitch, He threw my mas - ter

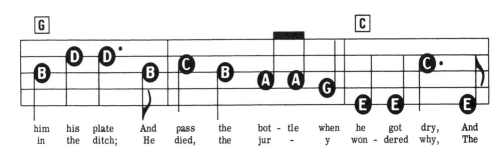

him his plate And pass the bot - tle when he got dry, And
in the ditch; He died, the jur - y won - dered why, The

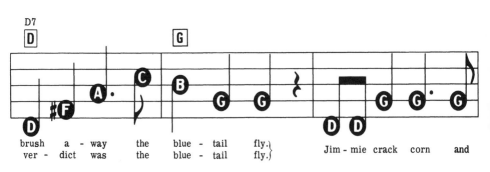

brush a - way the blue - tail fly. Jim - mie crack corn and
ver - dict was the blue - tail fly.

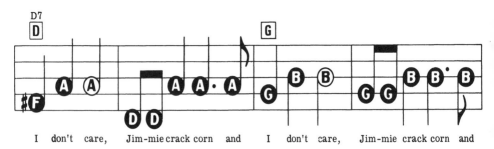

I don't care, Jim-mie crack corn and I don't care, Jim-mie crack corn and

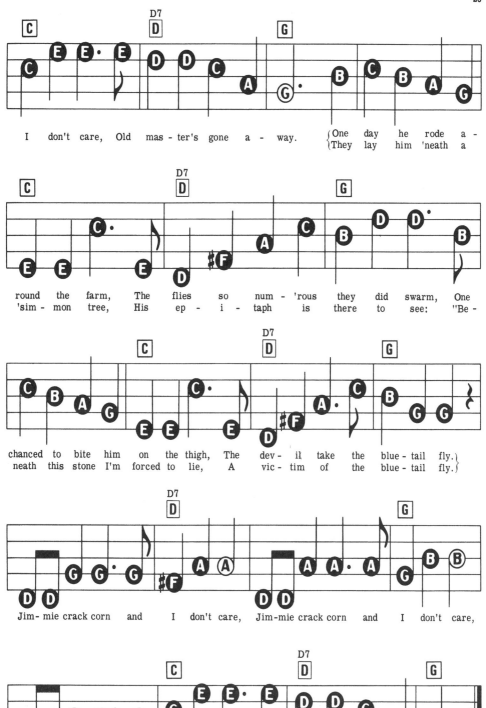

Bye, Baby Bunting

Registration 1
Rhythm: Waltz

Traditional

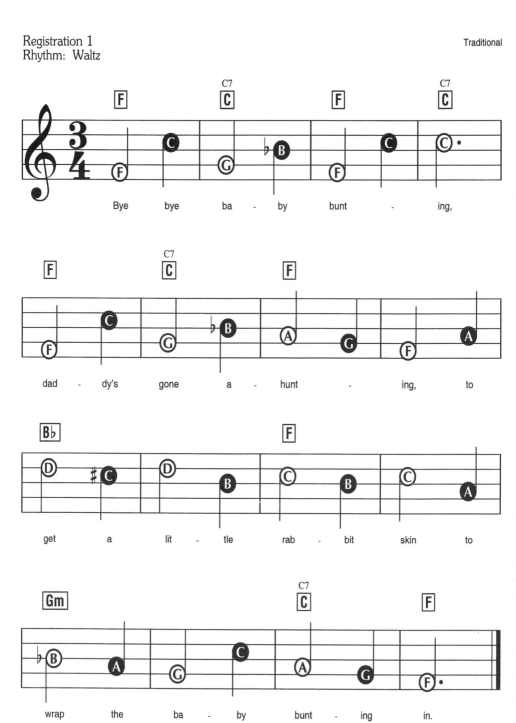

Bye bye ba - by bunt - ing,

dad - dy's gone a - hunt - ing, to

get a lit - tle rab - bit skin to

wrap the ba - by bunt - ing in.

(Oh, My Darling) Clementine

Registration 5
Rhythm: Waltz

Words and Music by
Percy Montrose

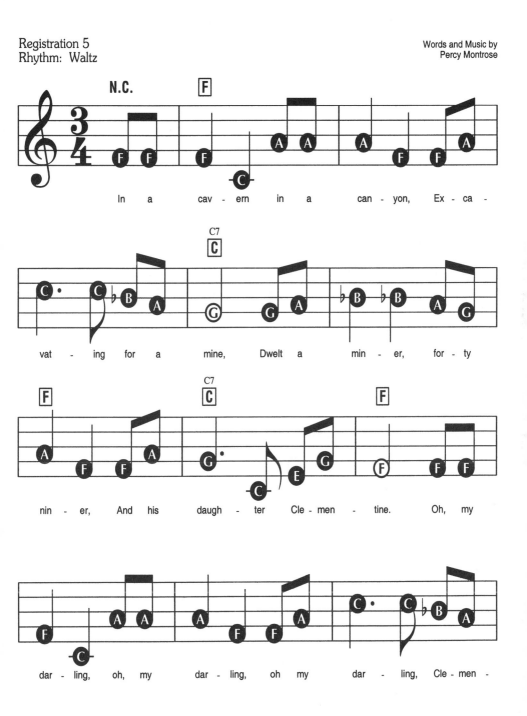

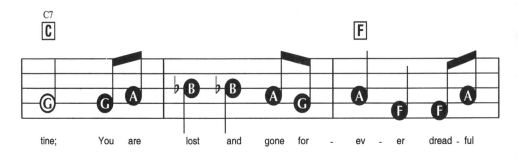

tine; You are lost and gone for - ev - er dread - ful

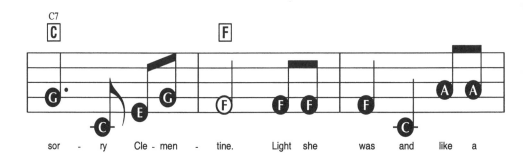

sor - ry Cle - men - tine. Light she was and like a

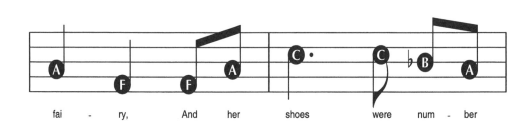

fai - ry, And her shoes were num - ber

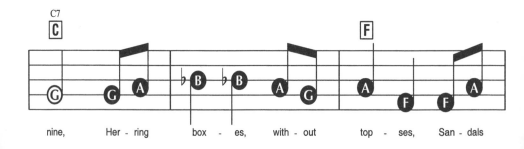

nine, Her - ring box - es, with - out top - ses, San - dals

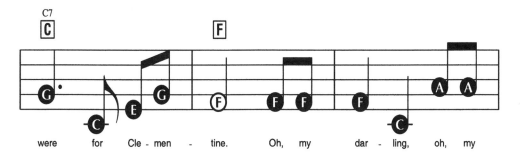

were for Cle - men - tine. Oh, my dar - ling, oh, my

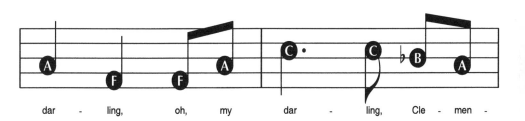

dar - ling, oh, my dar - ling, Cle - men -

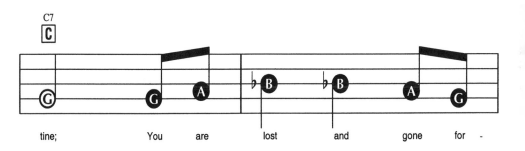

tine; You are lost and gone for -

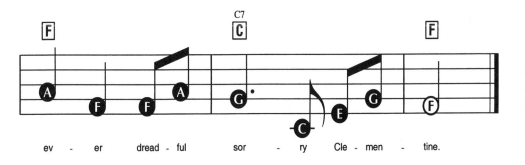

ev - er dread - ful sor - ry Cle - men - tine.

Cock-A-Doodle-Doo

Registration 3
Rhythm: Waltz

Traditional

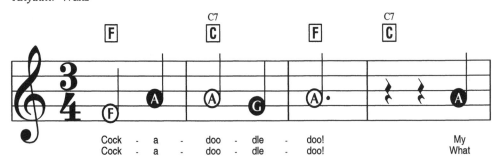

Cock - a - doo - dle - doo!   My
Cock - a - doo - dle - doo!   What

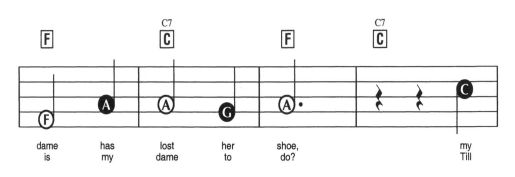

dame   has   lost   her   shoe,   my
is   my   dame   to   do?   Till

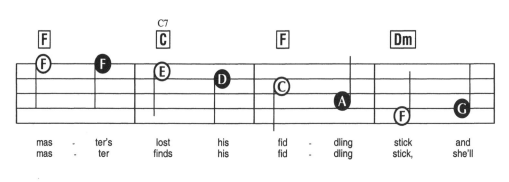

mas - ter's   lost   his   fid - dling   stick,   and
mas - ter   finds   his   fid - dling   stick,   she'll

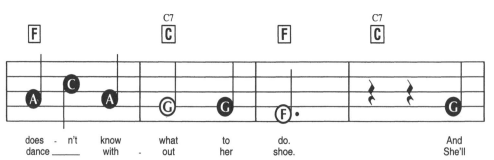

does - n't   know   what   to   do.   And
dance ___ with - out   her   shoe.   She'll

29

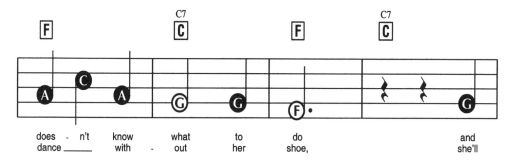

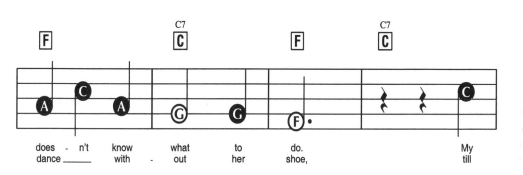

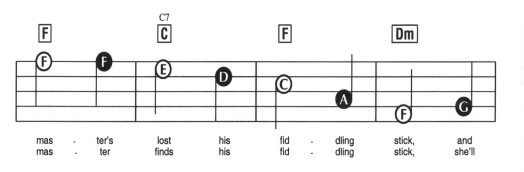

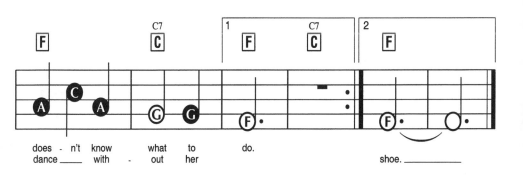

Do Your Ears Hang Low?

Registration 1
Rhythm: Fox Trot or March

Traditional

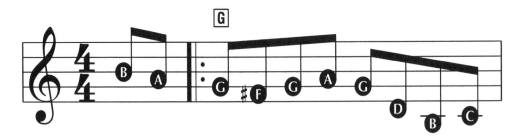

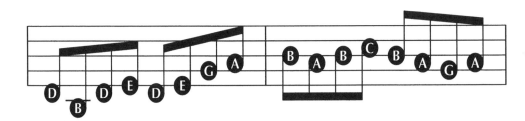

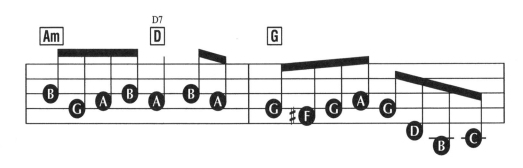

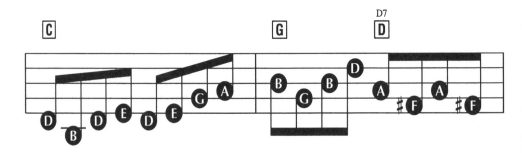

Down by the Station

Registration 2
Rhythm: March or Polka

Traditional

Down   by   the   sta - tion,   ear - ly   in   the   morn - ing,

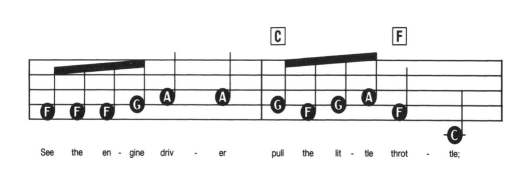

see   the   lit - tle   puf - fer   bel - lies   all   in   a   row.

See   the   en - gine   driv - er   pull   the   lit - tle   throt - tle;

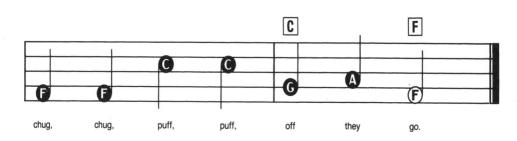

chug,   chug,   puff,   puff,   off   they   go.

Dry Bones

Registration 3
Rhythm: Folk or Fox Trot

Traditional

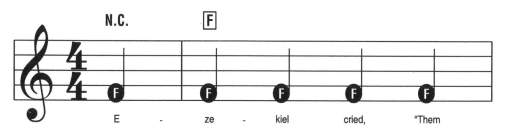

E - ze - kiel   cried,   "Them

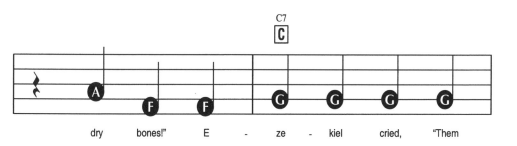

dry   bones!"   E - ze - kiel   cried,   "Them

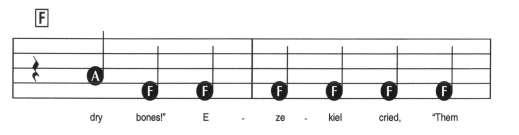

dry   bones!"   E - ze - kiel   cried,   "Them

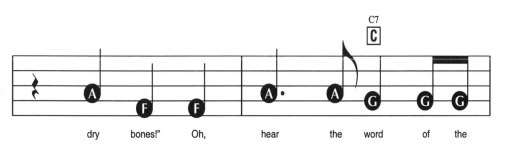

dry   bones!"   Oh,   hear   the   word   of   the

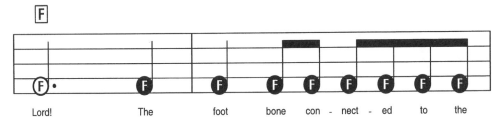

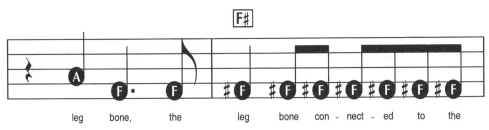

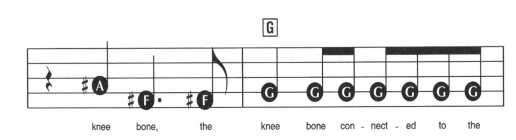

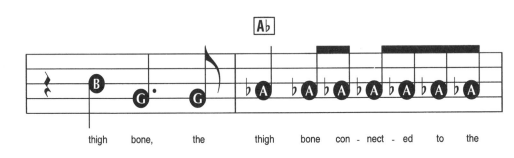

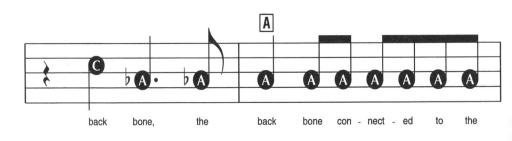

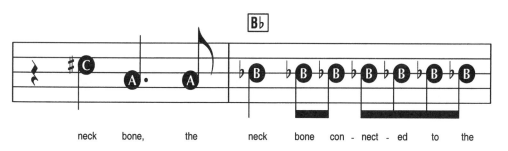

neck bone, the neck bone con - nect - ed to the

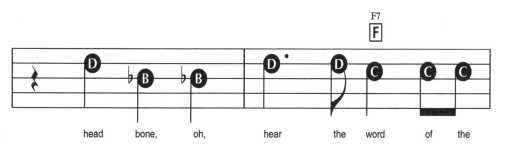

head bone, oh, hear the word of the

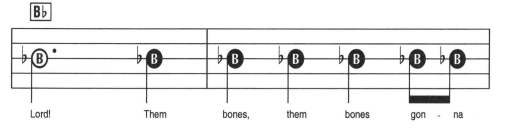

Lord! Them bones, them bones gon - na

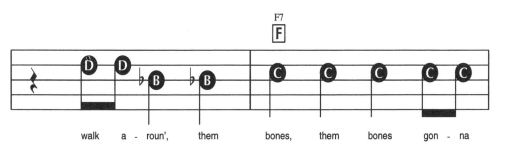

walk a - roun', them bones, them bones gon - na

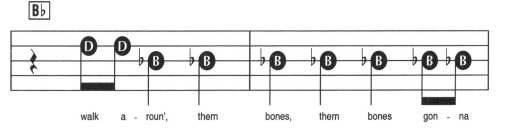

walk a - roun', them bones, them bones gon - na

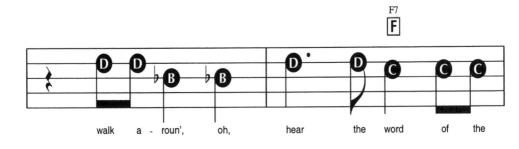

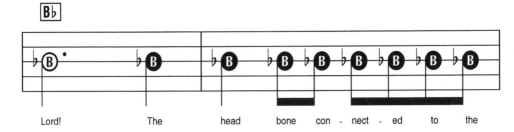

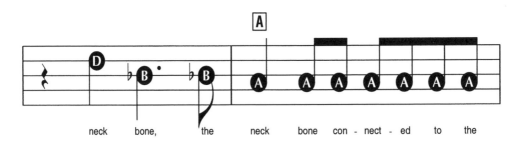

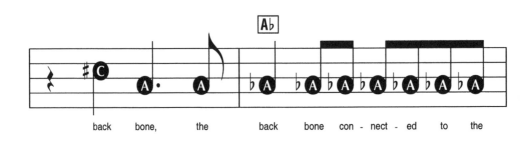

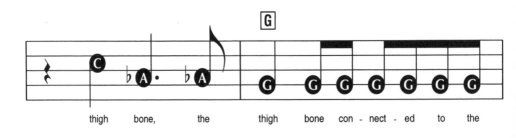

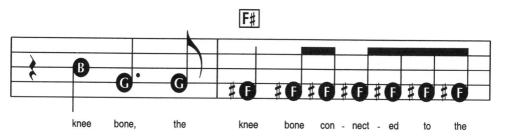

knee bone, the knee bone con - nect - ed to the

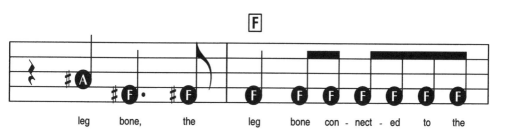

leg bone, the leg bone con - nect - ed to the

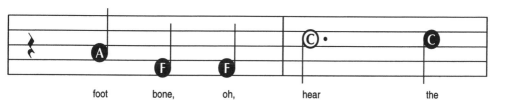

foot bone, oh, hear the

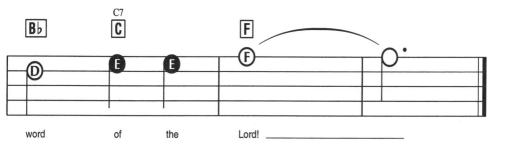

word of the Lord! _____

Down in My Heart

Registration 3
Rhythm: Fox Trot

Traditional

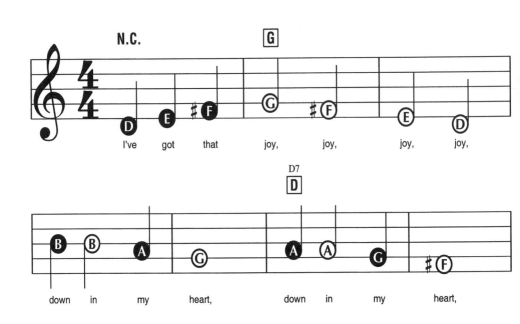

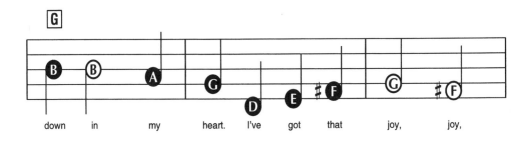

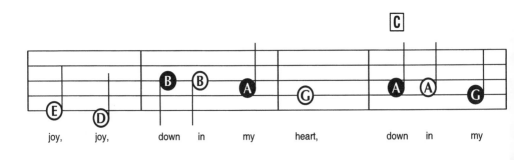

39

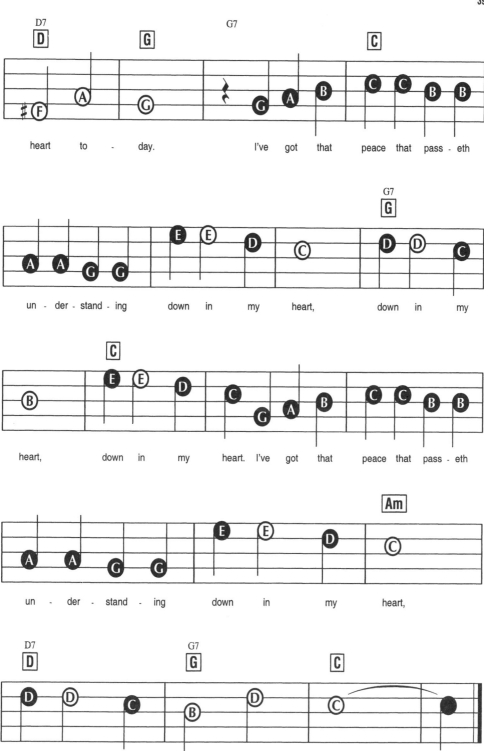

Eensy Weensy Spider

Registration 8
Rhythm: Waltz

Traditional

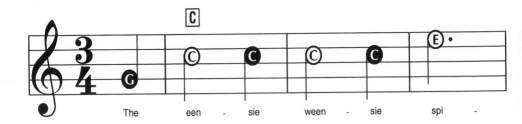

The een - sie ween - sie spi -

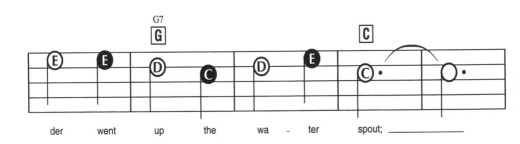

der went up the wa - ter spout; _____

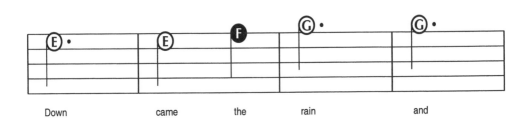

Down came the rain and

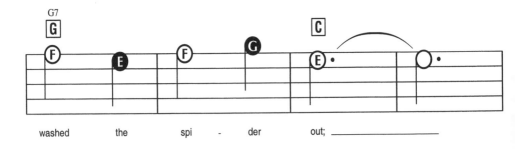

washed the spi - der out; _____

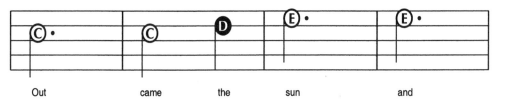

Out came the sun and

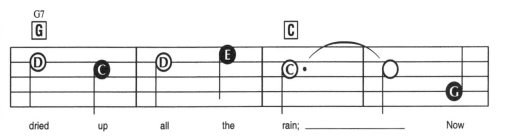

dried up all the rain; _____ Now

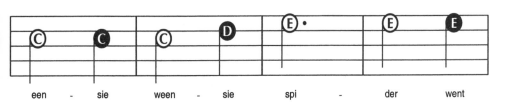

een - sie ween - sie spi - der went

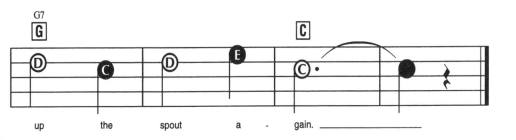

up the spout a - gain. _____

Evening Prayer

from HANSEL AND GRETEL

Registration 1
Rhythm: Fox Trot

By Engelbert Humperdinck

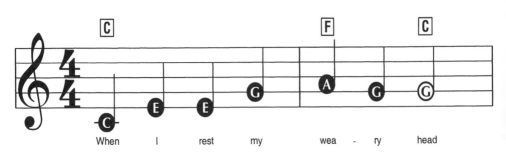

When I rest my wea - ry head

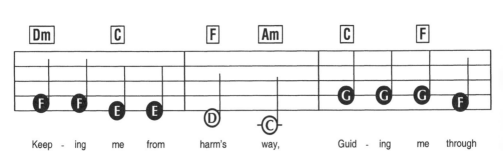

an - gels gath - er 'round my _____ bed;

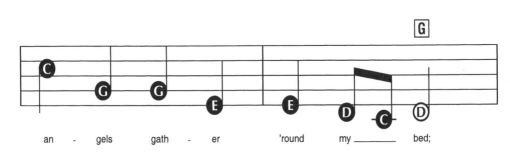

Keep - ing me from harm's way, Guid - ing me through

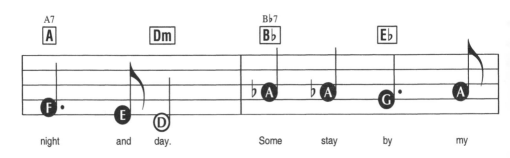

night and day. Some stay by my

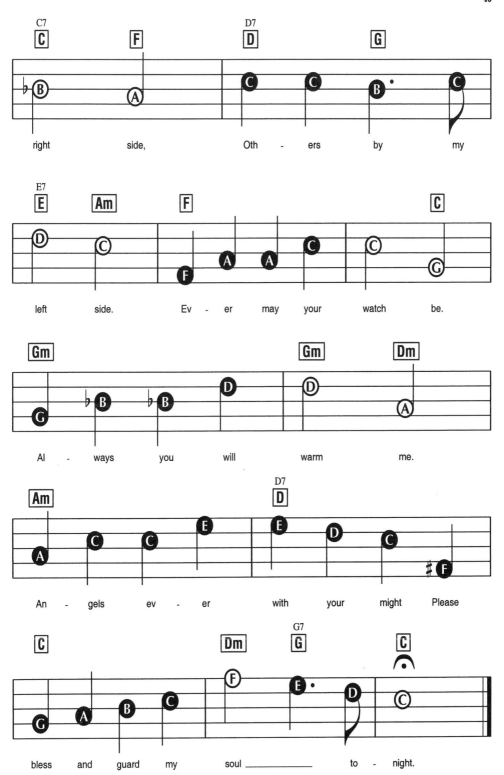

The Farmer in the Dell

Registration 3
Rhythm: Waltz

Traditional

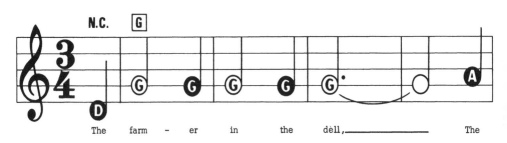

The farm - er in the dell,＿＿＿＿ The

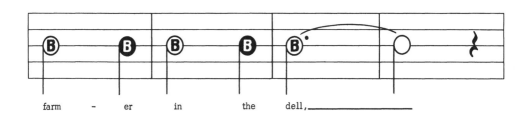

farm - er in the dell,＿＿＿＿

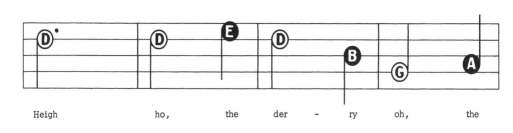

Heigh ho, the der - ry oh, the

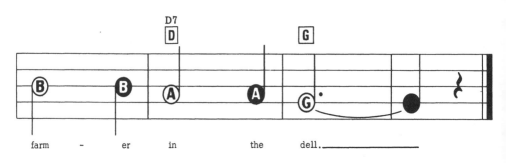

farm - er in the dell.＿＿＿＿

Frère Jacques
(Are You Sleeping?)

Registration 4
Rhythm: Fox Trot or Swing

Traditional

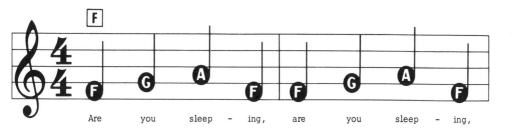

Are   you   sleep – ing,   are   you   sleep – ing,

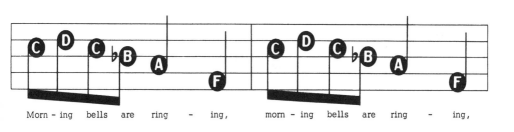

broth – er   John,   broth – er   John?

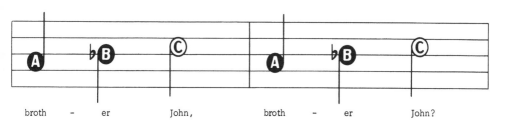

Morn – ing   bells   are   ring – ing,   morn – ing   bells   are   ring – ing,

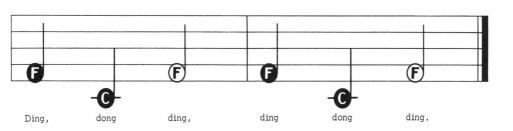

Ding,   dong   ding,   ding   dong   ding.

For He's a Jolly Good Fellow

Registration 4
Rhythm: Waltz

Traditional

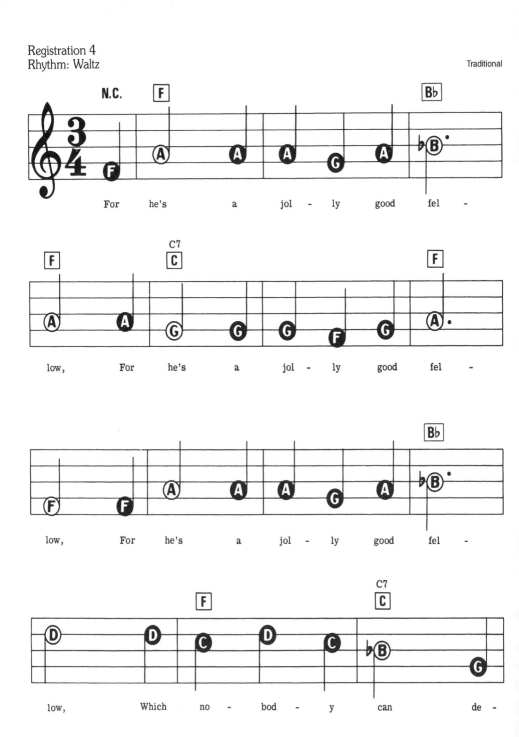

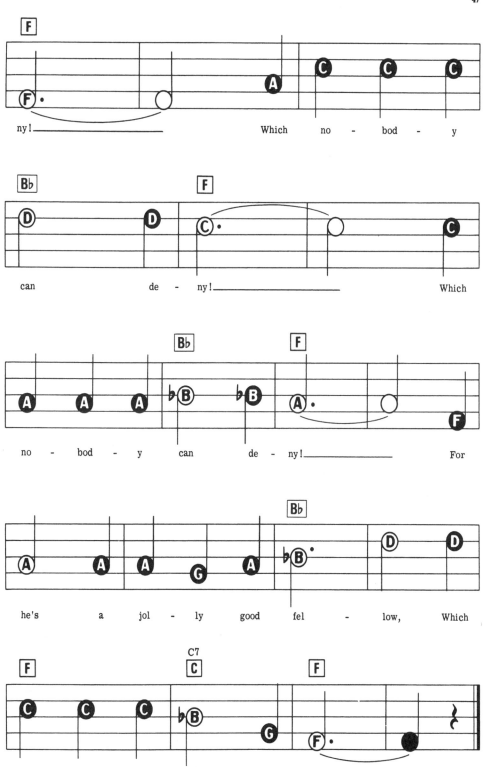

Frog Went A-Courtin'

Registration 2
Rhythm: March, Polka or Pops

Traditional

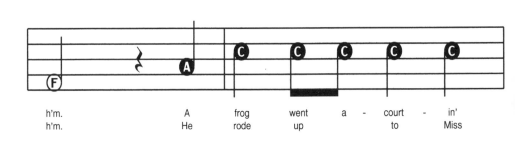

1. A   frog   went   a -   court -   in',
2. rode   up   to   Miss
3. - 9. *(See additional lyrics)*

he   did   ride.   H'm,   h'm,   h'm,
Mous - ie's   den.   H'm,   h'm,   h'm,

h'm.   A   frog   went   a -   court -   in'
h'm.   He   rode   up   to   Miss

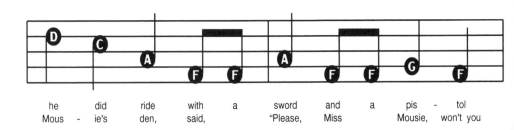

he   did   ride   with   a   sword   and   a   pis - tol
Mous - ie's   den,   said,   "Please,   Miss   Mousie,   won't you

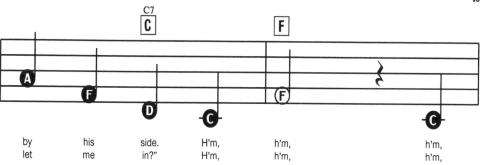

by   his   side.   H'm,   h'm,   h'm,
let   me   in?"   H'm,   h'm,   h'm,

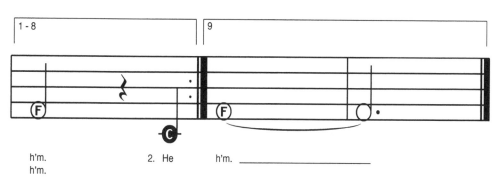

h'm.   2. He   h'm. _____
h'm.

Additional Lyrics

3. "Yes, Sir Frog, I sit and spin."
H'm, h'm, H'm, h'm.
"Yes, Sir Frog, I sit and spin;
Pray Mister Froggie, won't you walk in?"
H'm, h'm, H'm, h'm.

4. The frog said, "My dear, I've come to see."
H'm, h'm, H'm, h'm.
The frog said, "My dear, I've come to see
If you, Miss Mousie, will marry me."
H'm, h'm, H'm, h'm.

5. "I don't know what to say to that."
H'm, h'm, H'm, h'm.
"I don't know what to say to that
Till I speak with my Uncle Rat."
H'm, h'm, H'm, h'm.

6. When Uncle Rat came riding home,
H'm, h'm, H'm, h'm.
When Uncle Rat came riding home,
Said he, "Who's been here since I've been gone?"
H'm, h'm, H'm, h'm.

7. "A fine young froggie has been here."
H'm, h'm, H'm, h'm.
"A fine young froggie has been here;
He means to marry me, it's clear."
H'm, h'm, H'm, h'm.

8. So Uncle Rat, he rode to town.
H'm, h'm, H'm, h'm.
So Uncle Rat, he rode to town
And bought his niece a wedding gown.
H'm, h'm, H'm, h'm.

9. The frog and mouse they went to France.
H'm, h'm, H'm, h'm.
The frog and mouse they went to France,
And that's the end of my romance.
H'm, h'm, H'm, h'm.

Git Along, Little Dogies

Registration 3
Rhythm: Waltz

Western American Cowboy Song

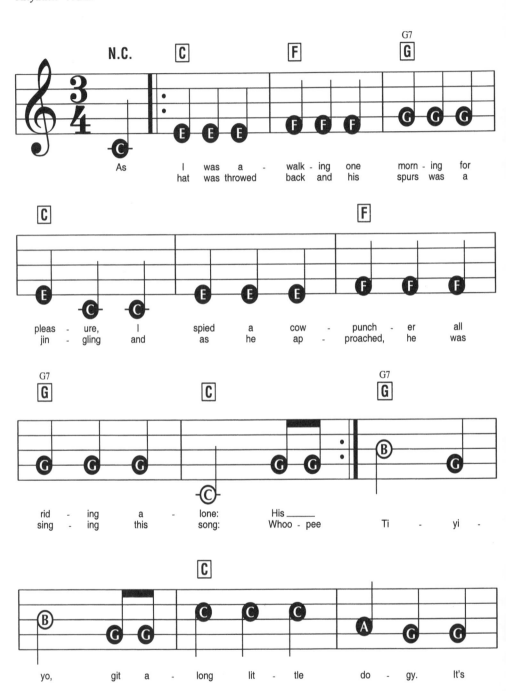

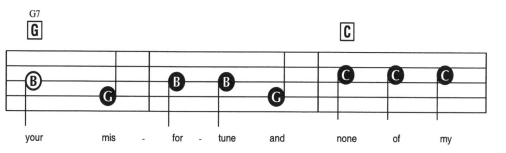

your mis - for - tune and none of my

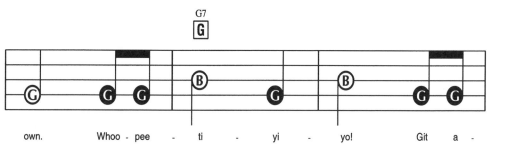

own. Whoo - pee - ti - yi - yo! Git a -

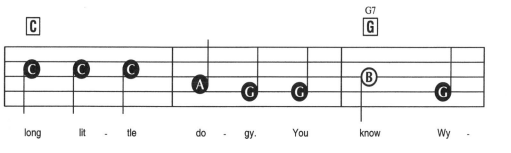

long lit - tle do - gy. You know Wy -

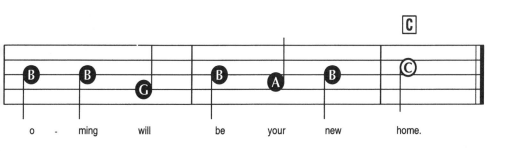

o - ming will be your new home.

Go Tell Aunt Rhody

Registration 4
Rhythm: Country or Fox Trot

Traditional

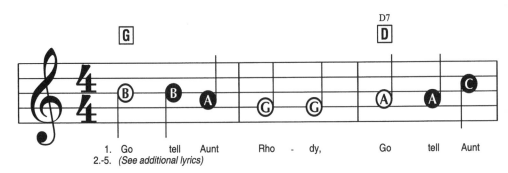

1. Go tell Aunt Rho - dy, Go tell Aunt
2.-5. *(See additional lyrics)*

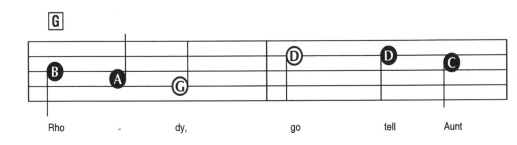

Rho - dy, go tell Aunt

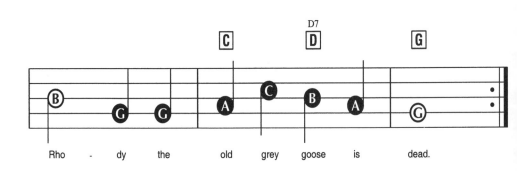

Rho - dy the old grey goose is dead.

Additional Lyrics

2. The one she was saving, *(three times)*
   To make a feather bed.

3. The gander is weeping, *(three times)*
   Because his wife is dead.

4. The goslings are crying, *(three times)*
   Because their mama's dead.

5. She died in the water, *(three times)*
   With her heels above her head.

Goosey, Goosey Gander

Registration 8
Rhythm: Fox Trot

Traditional

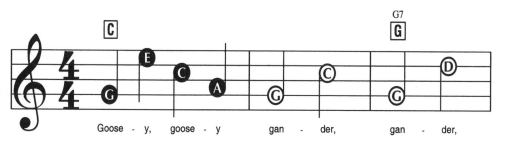

Goose - y, goose - y gan - der, gan - der,

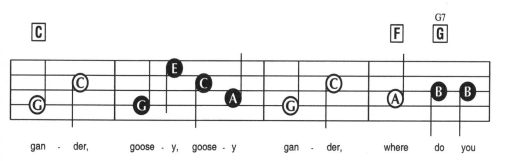

gan - der, goose - y, goose - y gan - der, where do you

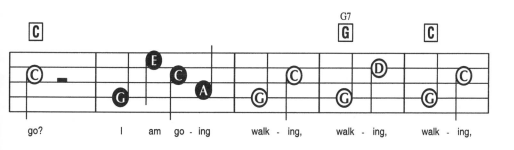

go? I am go - ing walk - ing, walk - ing, walk - ing,

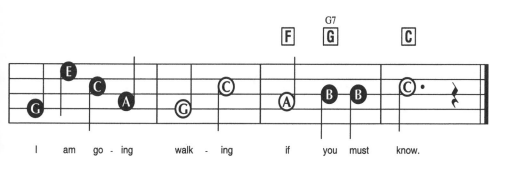

I am go - ing walk - ing if you must know.

Goober Peas

Registration 8
Rhythm: March

Words by P. Pindar
Music by P. Nutt

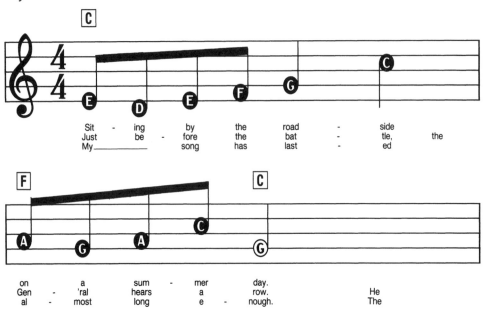

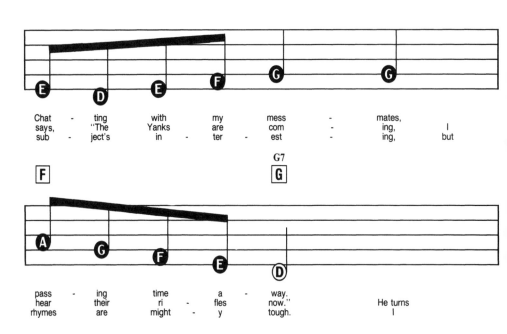

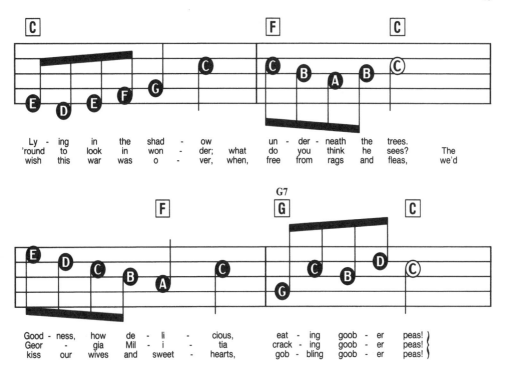

Ly - ing in the shad - ow un - der - neath the trees.
'round to look in won - der; what do you think he sees? The
wish this war was o - ver, when, free from rags and fleas, we'd

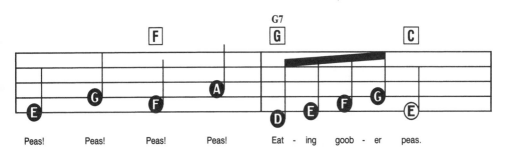

Good - ness, how de - li - cious, eat - ing goob - er peas!
Geor - gia Mil - i - tia crack - ing goob - er peas!
kiss our wives and sweet - hearts, gob - bling goob - er peas!

Peas! Peas! Peas! Peas! Eat - ing goob - er peas.

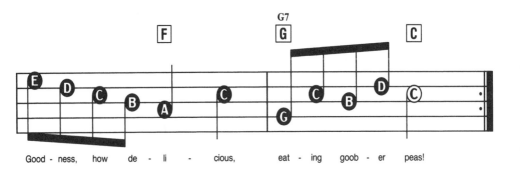

Good - ness, how de - li - cious, eat - ing goob - er peas!

Grandfather's Clock

Registration 7
Rhythm: Fox Trot

By Henry Clay Work

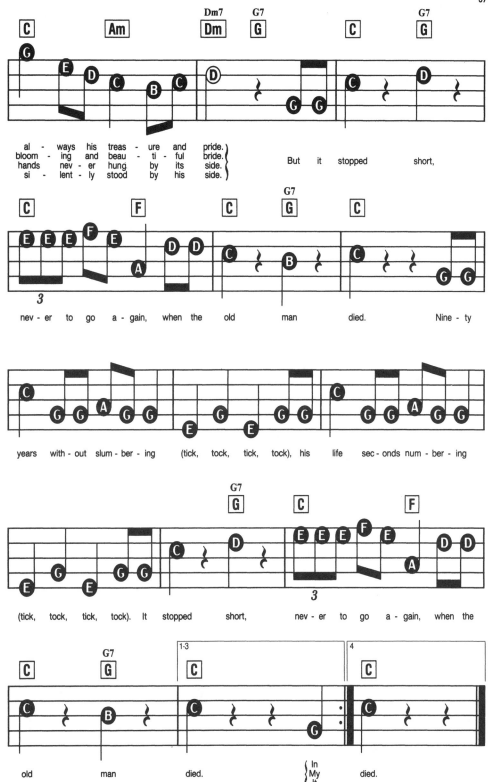

Hail, Hail, the Gang's All Here

Registration 2
Rhythm: 6/8 March

Traditional

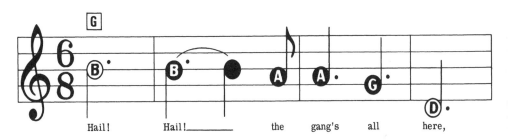

Hail! Hail!_____ the gang's all here,

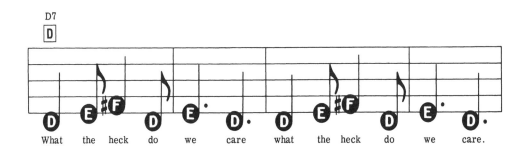

What the heck do we care what the heck do we care.

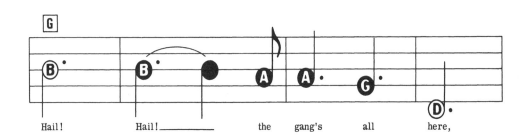

Hail! Hail!_____ the gang's all here,

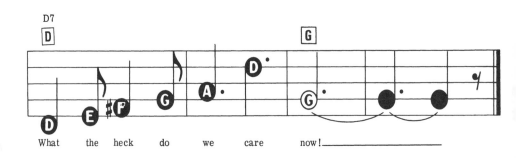

What the heck do we care now!_____

Hey Diddle Diddle

Registration 7
Rhythm: Waltz

Traditional

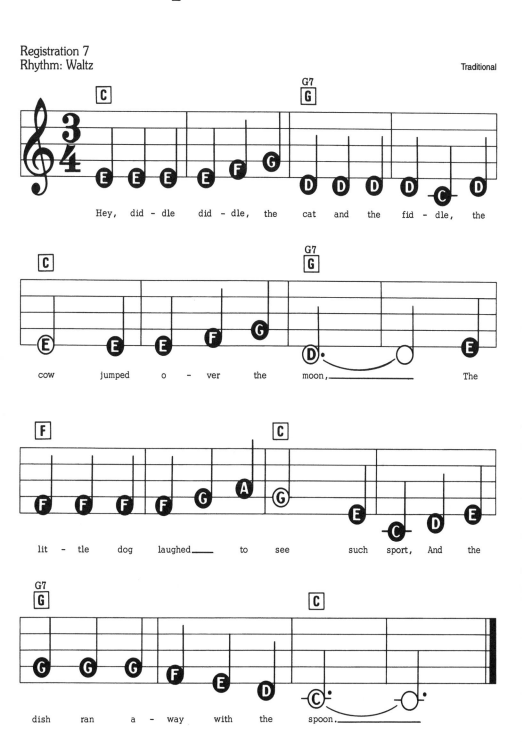

He's Got the Whole World in His Hands

Registration 1
Rhythm: Swing or Rock

Traditional Spiritual

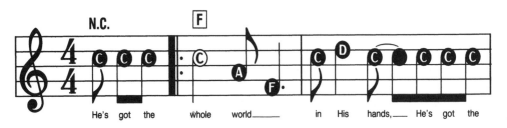

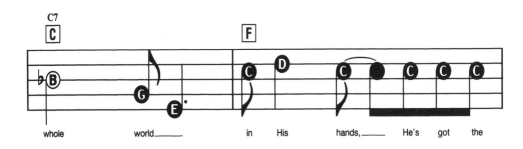

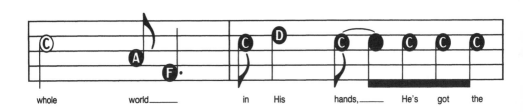

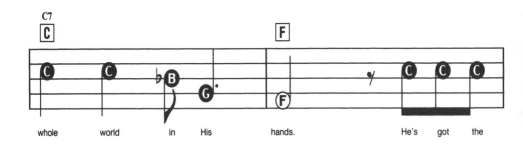

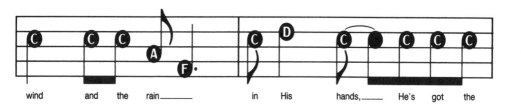

wind   and   the   rain_____   in   His   hands,_____   He's   got   the

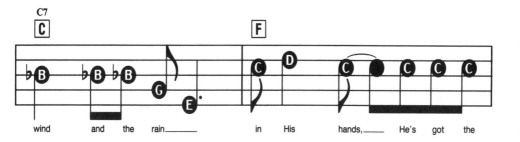

wind   and   the   rain_____   in   His   hands,_____   He's   got   the

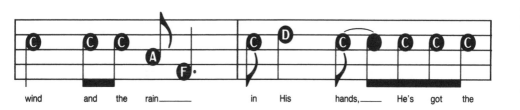

wind   and   the   rain_____   in   His   hands,_____   He's   got   the

Repeat and Fade

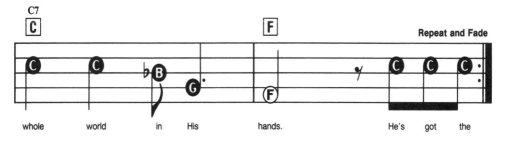

whole   world   in   His   hands.   He's   got   the

Hey, Ho! Nobody Home

Registration 1
Rhythm: Fox Trot

Traditional

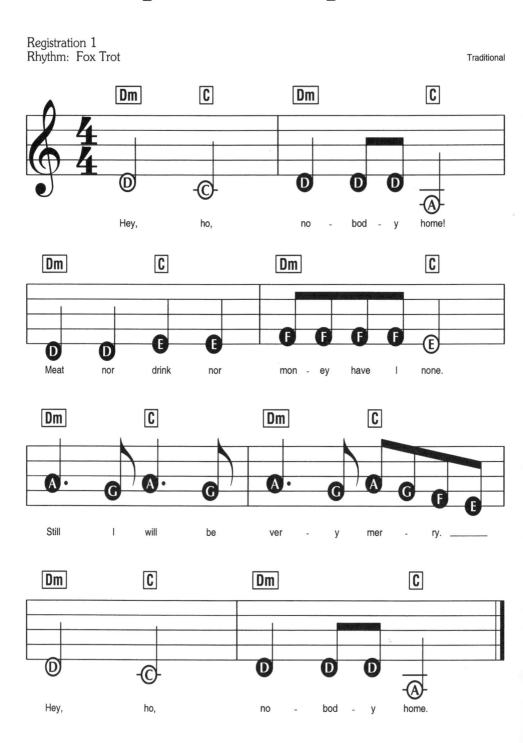

Hickory Dickory Dock

Registration 1
Rhythm: Waltz

Traditional

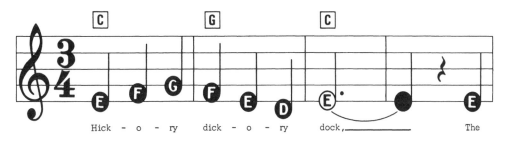

Hick - o - ry dick - o - ry dock,_____ The

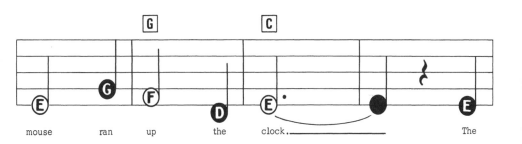

mouse ran up the clock._____ The

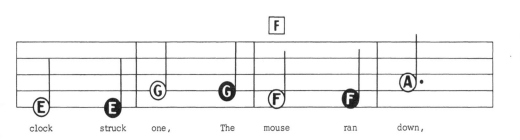

clock struck one, The mouse ran down,

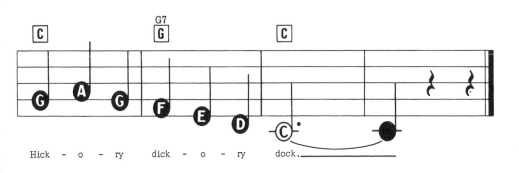

Hick - o - ry dick - o - ry dock._____

Home on the Range

Registration 4
Rhythm: Waltz

Lyrics by Dr. Brewster Higley
Music by Dan Kelly

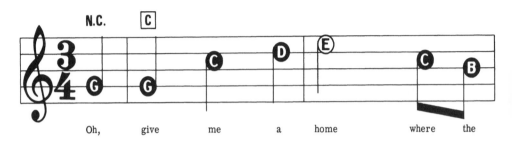

Oh, give me a home where the

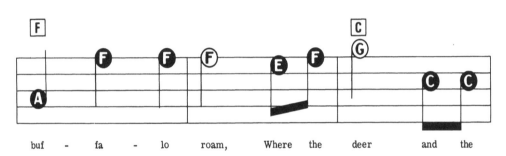

buf - fa - lo roam, Where the deer and the

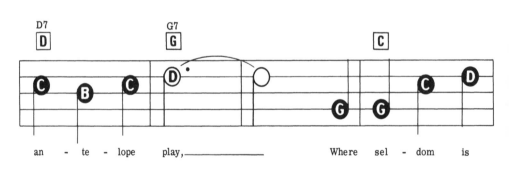

an - te - lope play,_____ Where sel - dom is

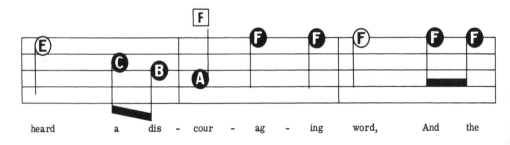

heard a dis - cour - ag - ing word, And the

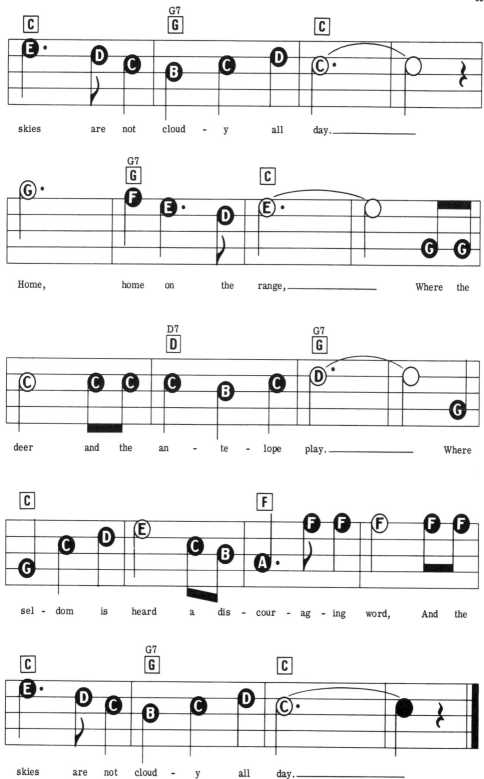

Hot Cross Buns

Registration 5
Rhythm: Fox Trot

Traditional

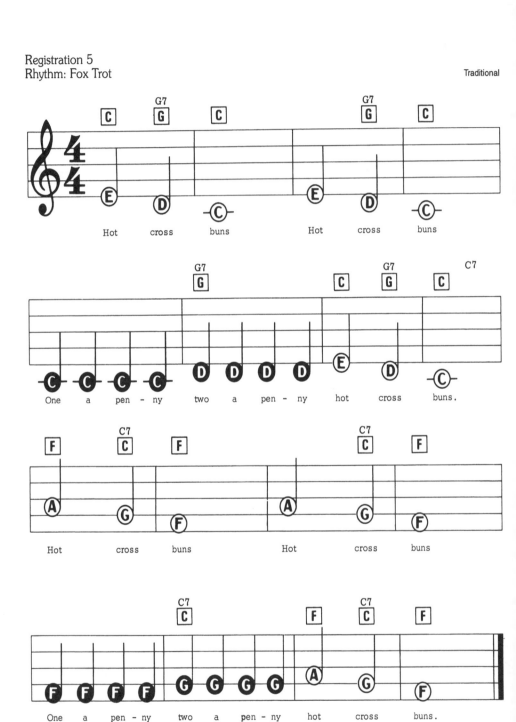

Humpty Dumpty

Registration 2
Rhythm: Waltz

Traditional

Hush, Little Baby

Registration 1
Rhythm: Fox Trot

Carolina Folk Lullaby

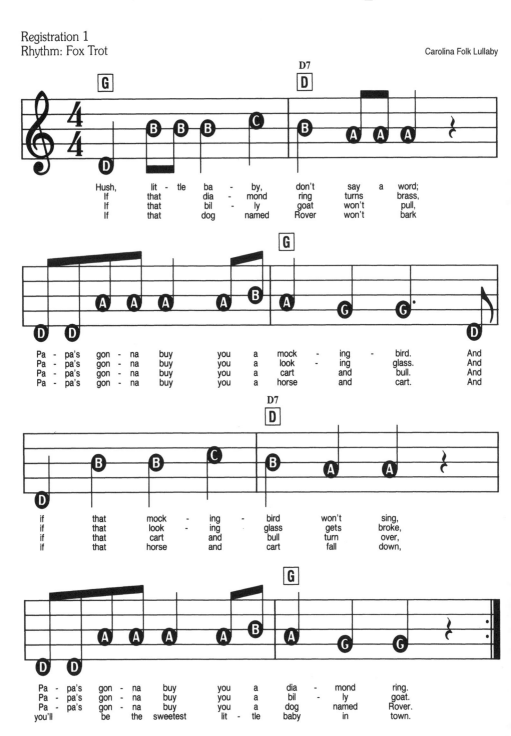

I've Been Working on the Railroad

Registration 5
Rhythm: March or Swing

American Folksong

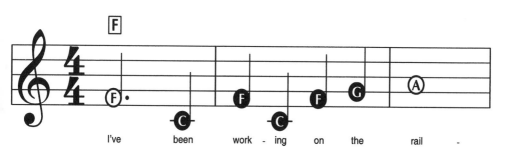

I've been work - ing on the rail -

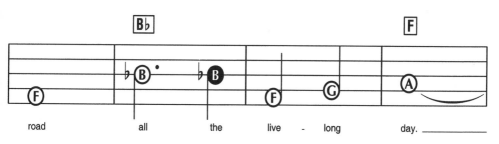

road all the live - long day.

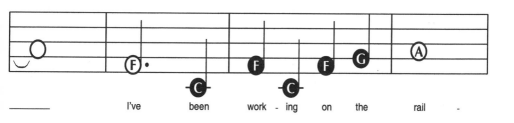

I've been work - ing on the rail -

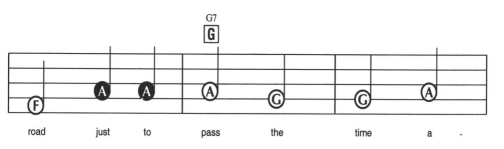

road just to pass the time a -

70

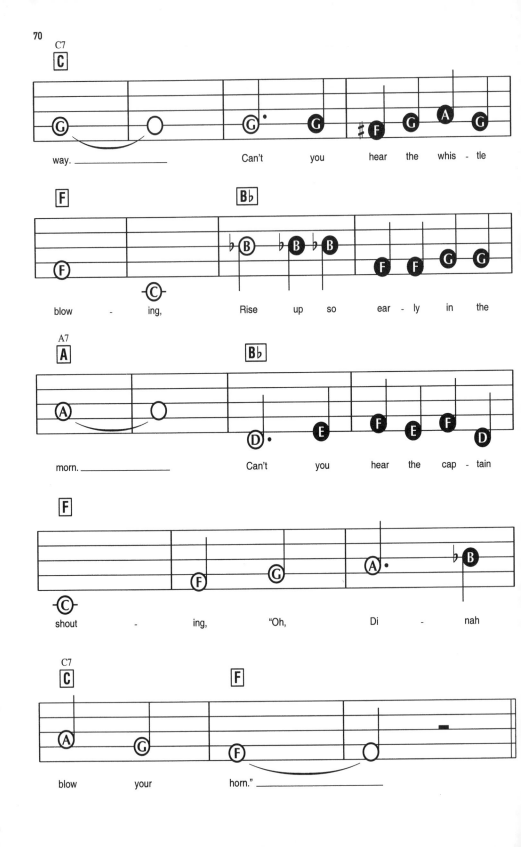

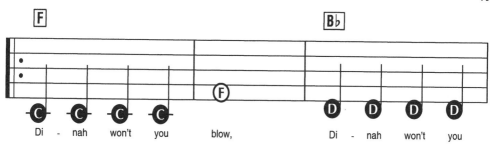

Di - nah won't you blow, Di - nah won't you

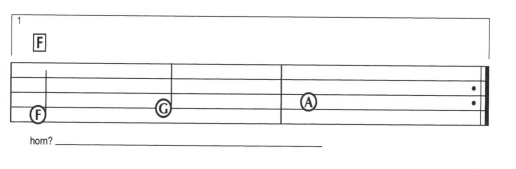

blow, Di - nah won't you blow your

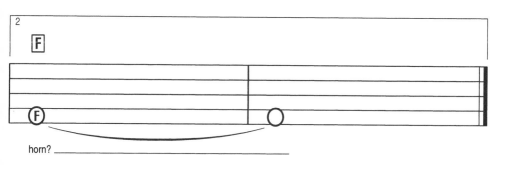

horn? _____

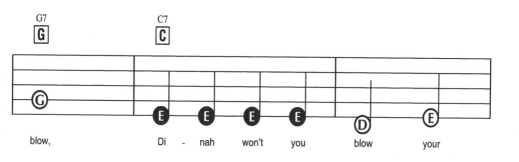

horn? _____

If You're Happy

(And You Know It)

Registration 4
Rhythm: Waltz

Words and Music by
L. Smith

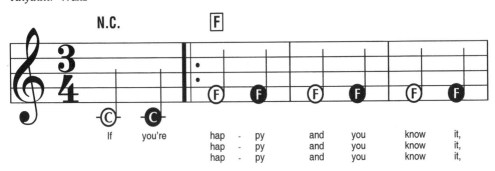

If you're hap - py and you know it,
hap - py and you know it,
hap - py and you know it,

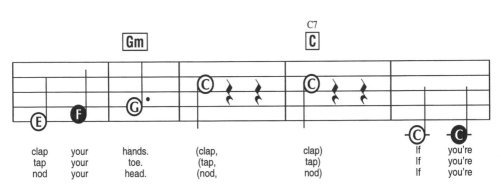

clap your hands. (clap, clap) If you're
tap your toe. (tap, tap) If you're
nod your head. (nod, nod) If you're

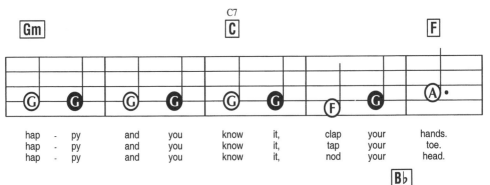

hap - py and you know it, clap your hands.
hap - py and you know it, tap your toe.
hap - py and you know it, nod your head.

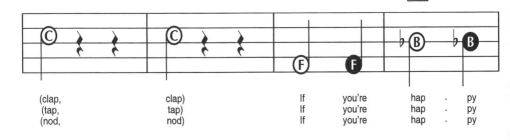

(clap, clap) If you're hap - py
(tap, tap) If you're hap - py
(nod, nod) If you're hap - py

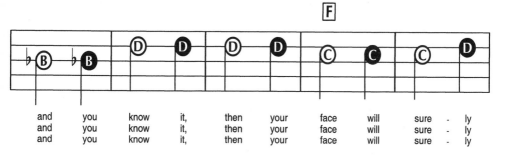

and	you	know	it,	then	your	face	will	sure	-	ly
and	you	know	it,	then	your	face	will	sure	-	ly
and	you	know	it,	then	your	face	will	sure	-	ly

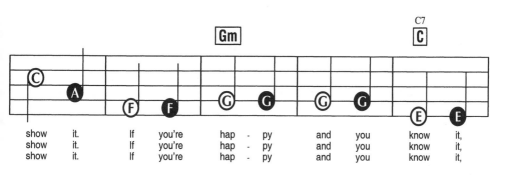

show	it.	If	you're	hap	-	py	and	you	know	it,
show	it.	If	you're	hap	-	py	and	you	know	it,
show	it.	If	you're	hap	-	py	and	you	know	it,

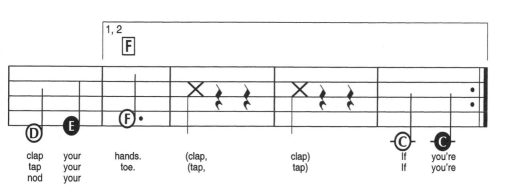

clap	your	hands.	(clap,	clap)	If	you're
tap	your	toe.	(tap,	tap)	If	you're
nod	your					

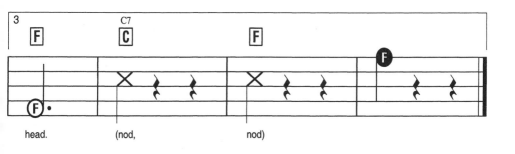

| head. | (nod, | nod) |

74

It's Raining, It's Pouring

Registration 1
Rhythm: Fox Trot

Traditional

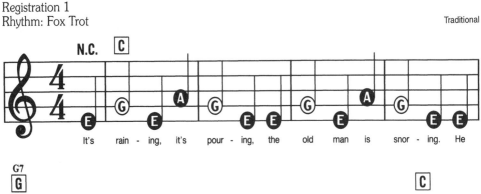

It's rain - ing, it's pour - ing, the old man is snor - ing. He

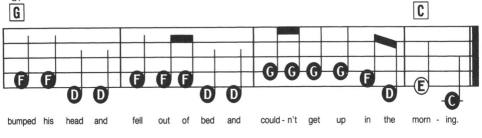

bumped his head and fell out of bed and could-n't get up in the morn - ing.

Ring Around the Rosie

Registration 2
Rhythm: 6/8 March

Traditional

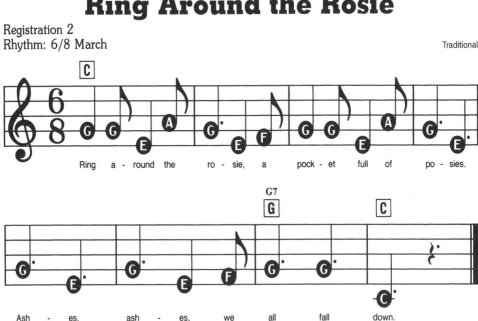

Ring a - round the ro - sie, a pock - et full of po - sies.

Ash - es, ash - es, we all fall down.

John Jacob Jingleheimer Schmidt

Registration 2
Rhythm: Polka or March

Traditional

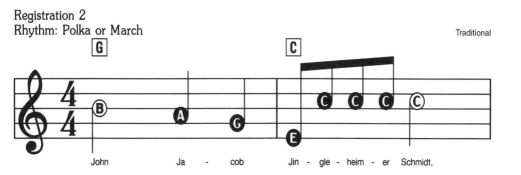

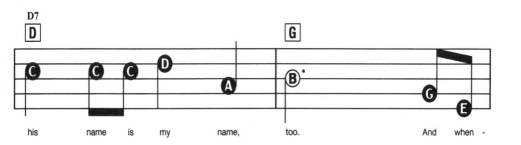

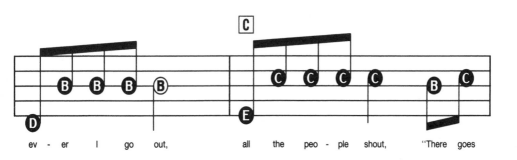

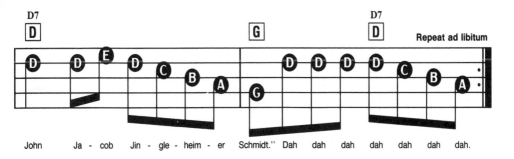

Jack and Jill

Registration 4
Rhythm: Waltz

Traditional

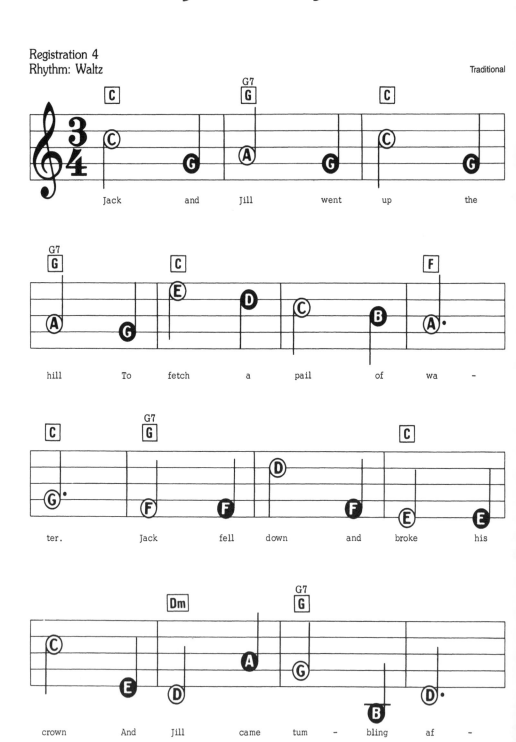

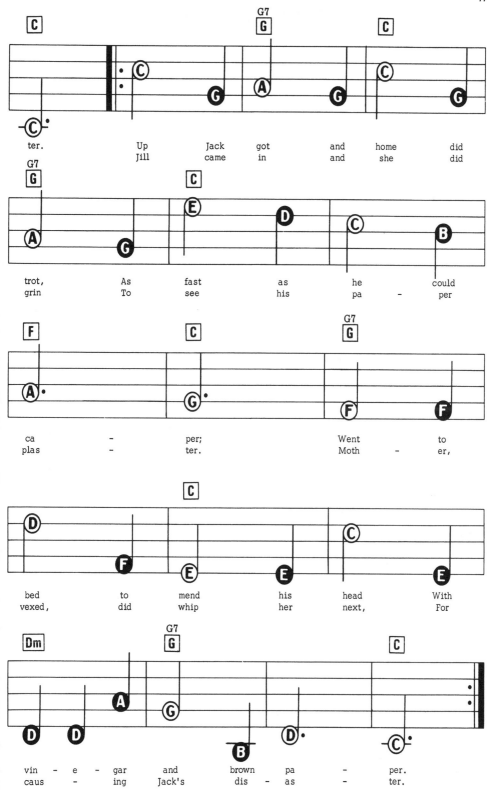

Jesus Loves Me

Registration 2
Rhythm: Gospel or Fox Trot

Words by Anna B. Warner
Music by William B. Bradbury

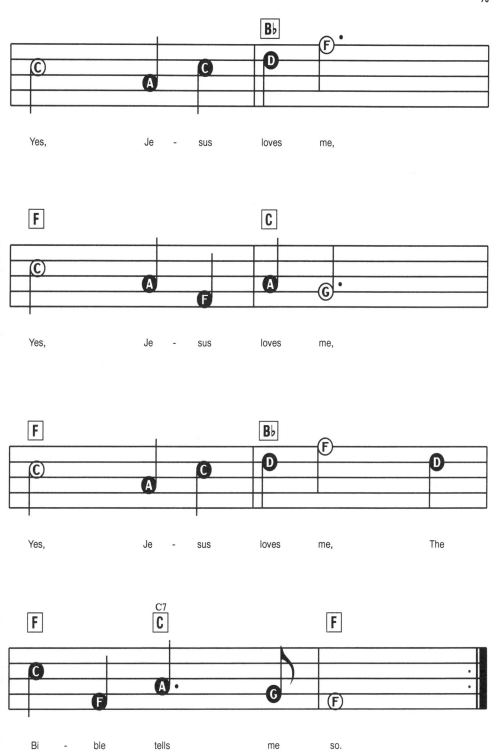

Yes,   Je - sus   loves   me,

Yes,   Je - sus   loves   me,

Yes,   Je - sus   loves   me,   The

Bi - ble   tells   me   so.

Kum Ba Yah

Registration 3
Rhythm: Rock

Traditional Spiritual

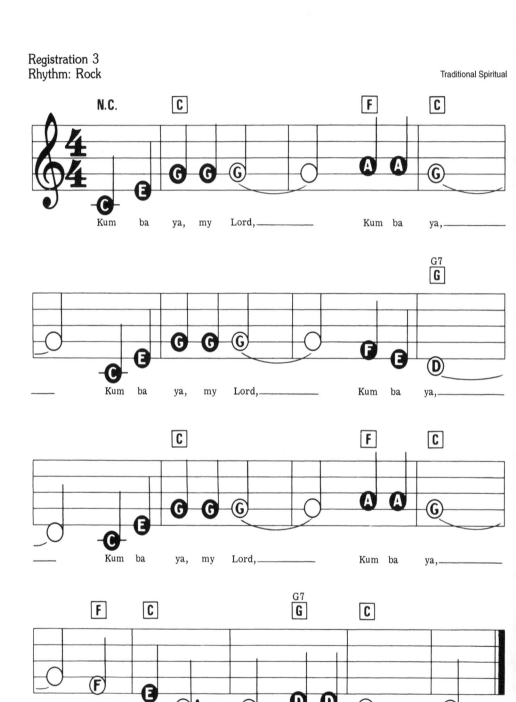

Lavender's Blue

Registration 3
Rhythm: Fox Trot or Swing

Traditional

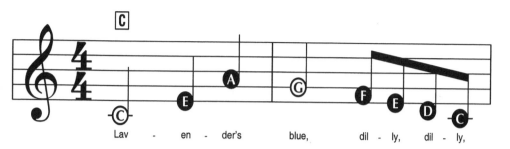

Lav - en - der's blue, dil - ly, dil - ly,

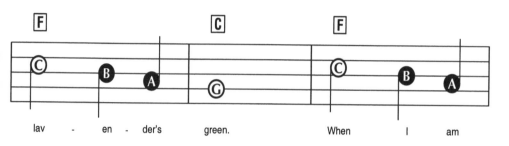

lav - en - der's green. When I am

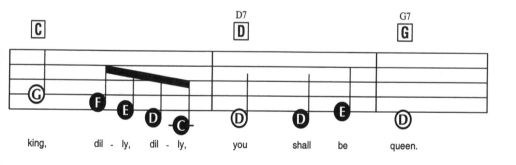

king, dil - ly, dil - ly, you shall be queen.

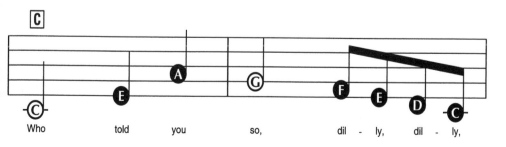

Who told you so, dil - ly, dil - ly,

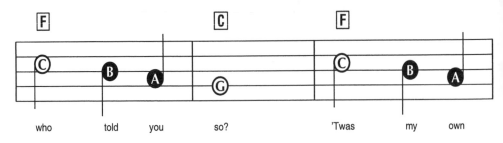

who told you so? 'Twas my own

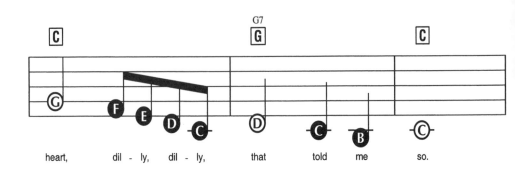

heart, dil - ly, dil - ly, that told me so.

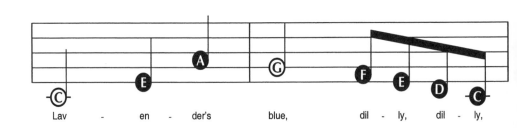

Lav - en - der's blue, dil - ly, dil - ly,

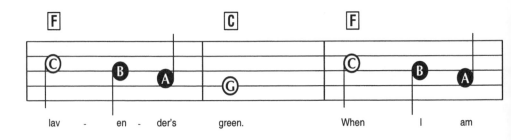

lav - en - der's green. When I am

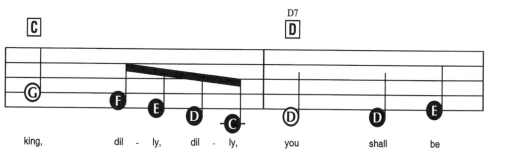

king, dil - ly, dil - ly, you shall be

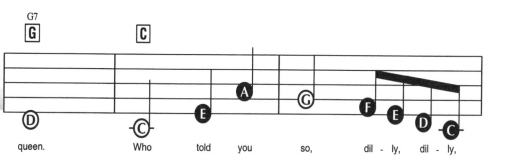

queen. Who told you so, dil - ly, dil - ly,

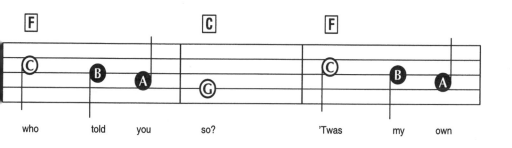

who told you so? 'Twas my own

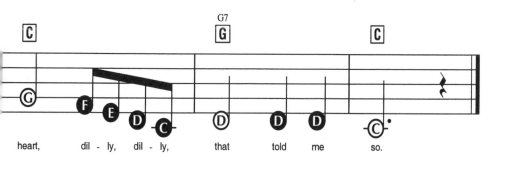

heart, dil - ly, dil - ly, that told me so.

Lazy Mary, Will You Get Up?

Registration 6
Rhythm: Waltz

Traditional

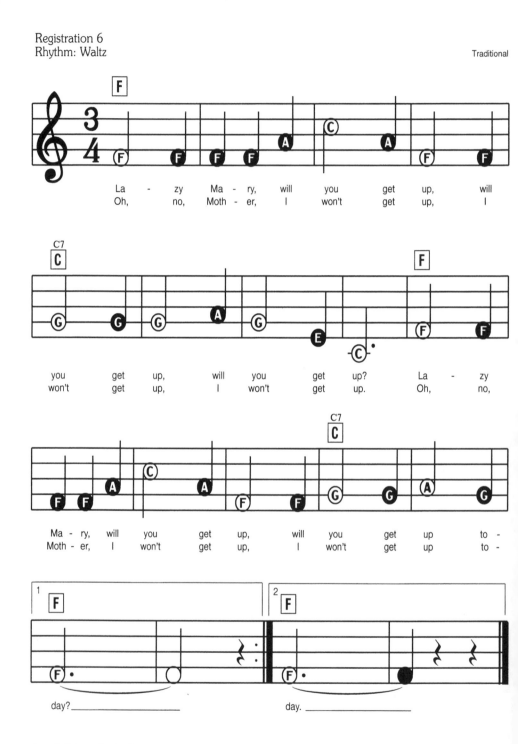

La - zy Ma - ry, will you get up, will
Oh, no, Moth - er, I won't get up, I

you get up, will you get up? La - zy
won't get up, I won't get up. Oh, no,

Ma - ry, will you get up, will you get up to -
Moth - er, I won't get up, I won't get up to -

day? _____
day. _____

Little Boy Blue

Registration 9
Rhythm: Waltz

Traditional

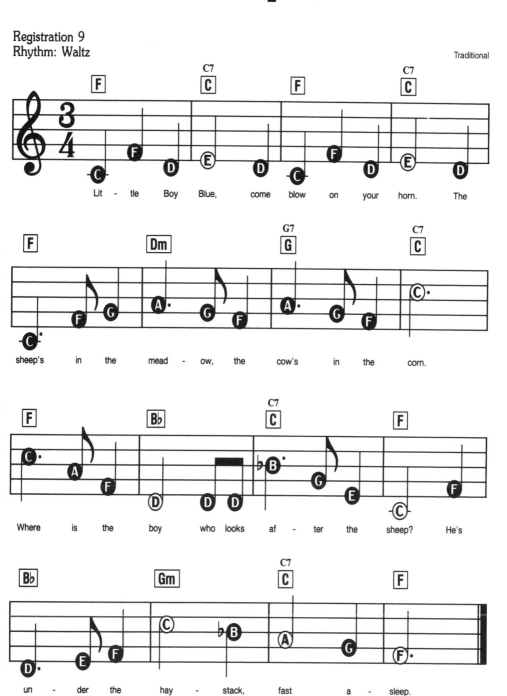

Little Bo-Peep

Registration 2
Rhythm: Waltz

Traditional

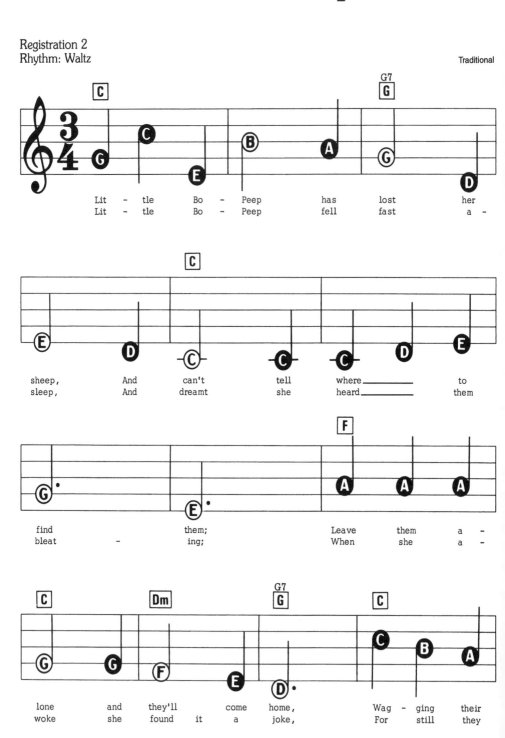

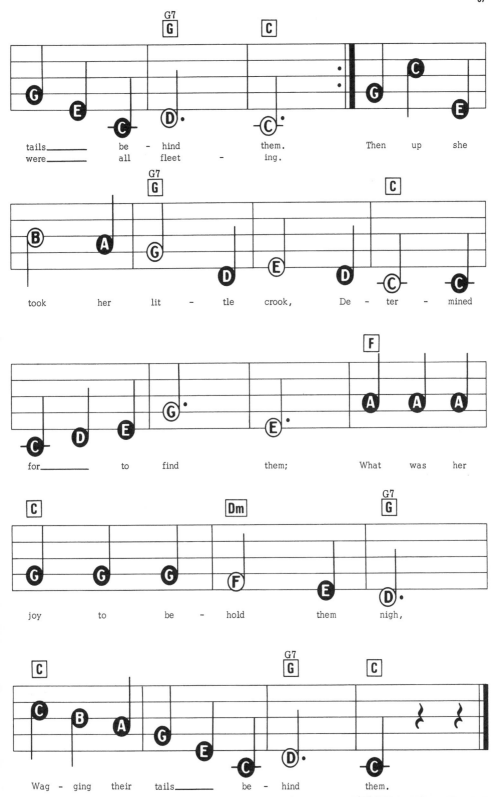

Little Jack Horner

Registration 1
Rhythm: Waltz

Traditional

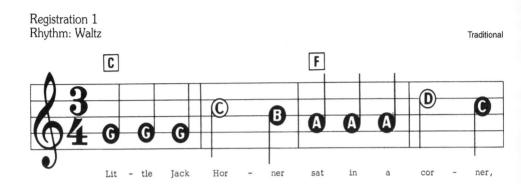

Lit - tle Jack Hor - ner sat in a cor - ner,

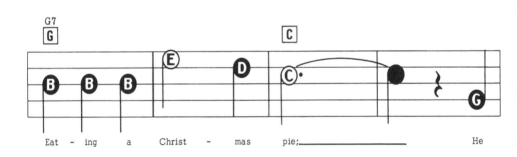

Eat - ing a Christ - mas pie;_____ He

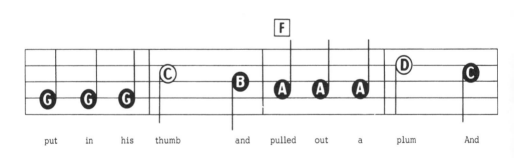

put in his thumb and pulled out a plum And

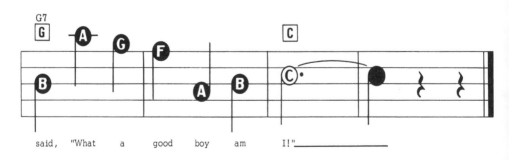

said, "What a good boy am I!"_____

Little Miss Muffet

Registration 8
Rhythm: Waltz

Traditional

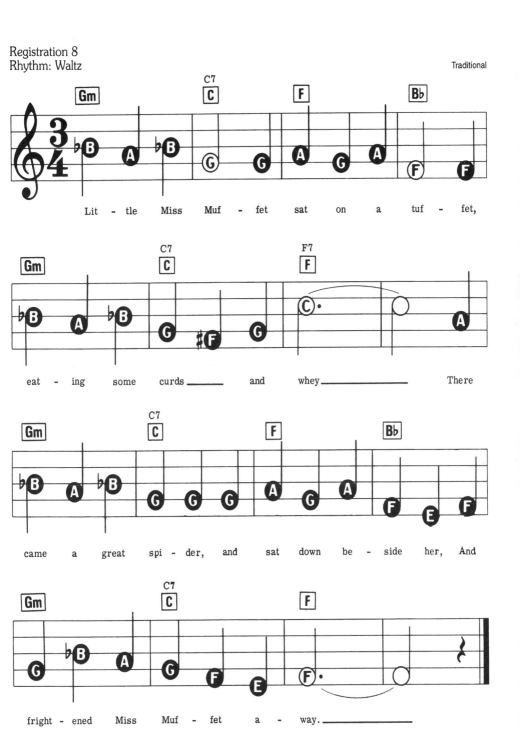

London Bridge

Registration 8
Rhythm: Fox Trot

Traditional

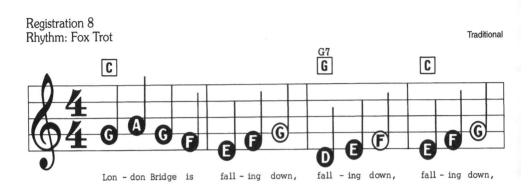

Lon - don Bridge is fall - ing down, fall - ing down, fall - ing down,

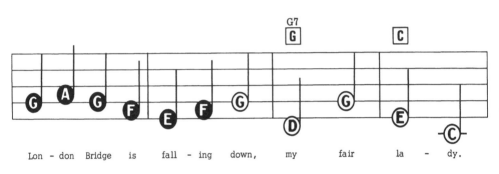

Lon - don Bridge is fall - ing down, my fair la - dy.

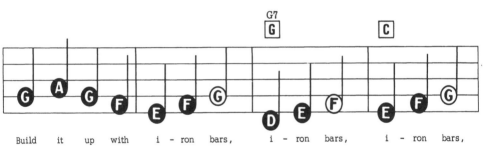

Build it up with i - ron bars, i - ron bars, i - ron bars,

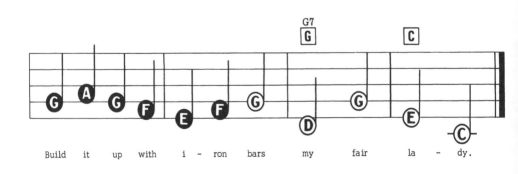

Build it up with i - ron bars my fair la - dy.

Michael Row the Boat Ashore

Registration 2
Rhythm: Swing

Traditional Folksong

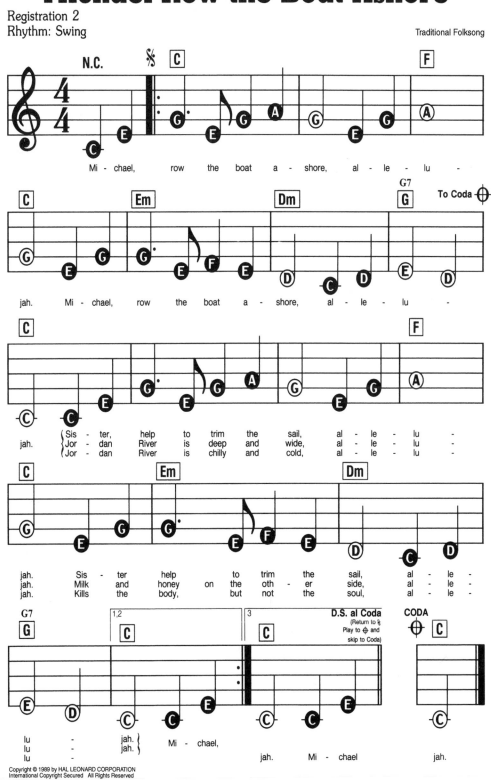

The Man on the Flying Trapeze

Registration 5
Rhythm: Waltz

Words by George Leybourne
Music by Alfred Lee

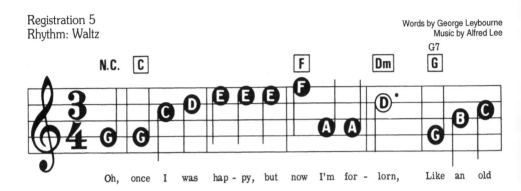

Oh, once I was hap-py, but now I'm for-lorn, Like an old

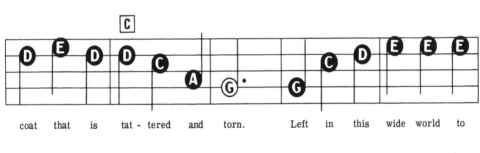

coat that is tat-tered and torn. Left in this wide world to

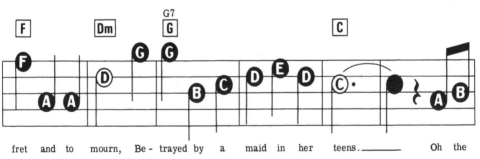

fret and to mourn, Be-trayed by a maid in her teens._____ Oh the

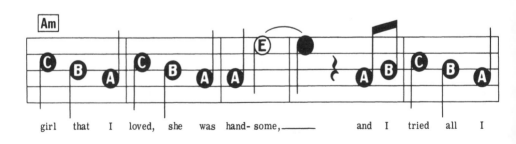

girl that I loved, she was hand-some,_____ and I tried all I

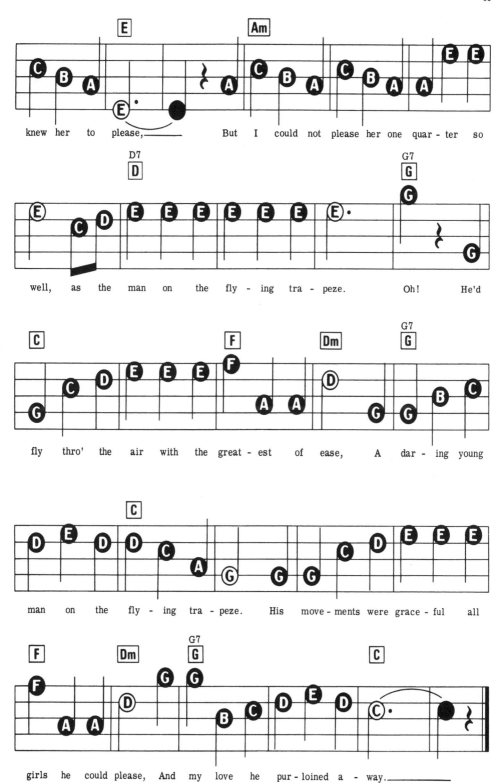

Mary Had a Little Lamb

Registration 4
Rhythm: Fox Trot or Swing

Words by Sarah Josepha Hale
Traditional Music

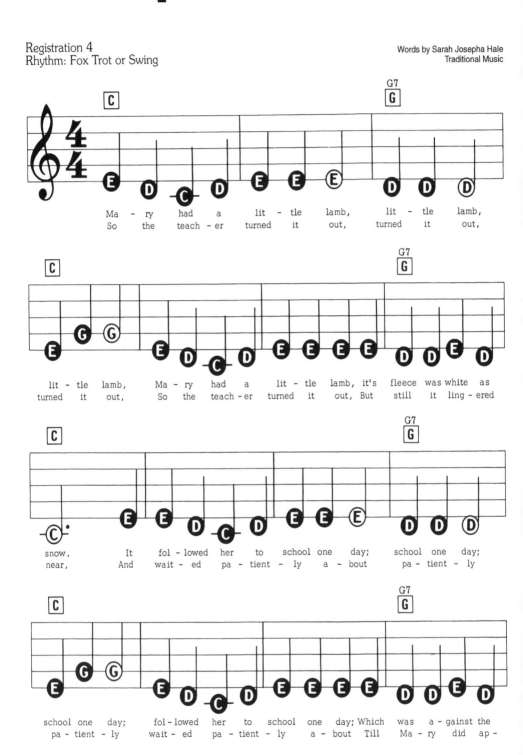

95

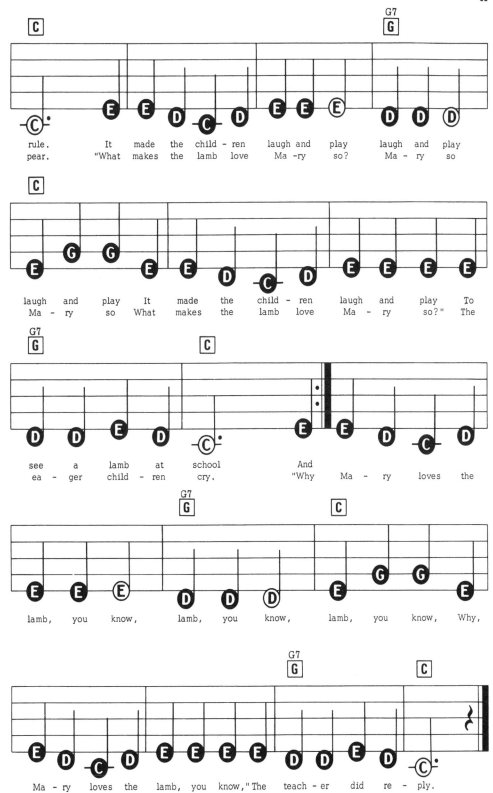

Mister Rabbit

Registration 4
Rhythm: Folk or Fox Trot

Traditional

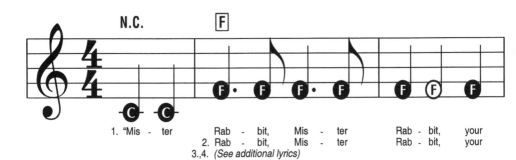

1. "Mis - ter   Rab - bit,   Mis - ter   Rab - bit,   your
2. Rab - bit,   Mis - ter   Rab - bit,   your
3.,4. *(See additional lyrics)*

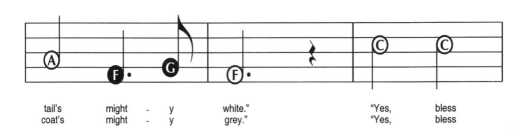

tail's   might - y   white."   "Yes,   bless
coat's   might - y   grey."   "Yes,   bless

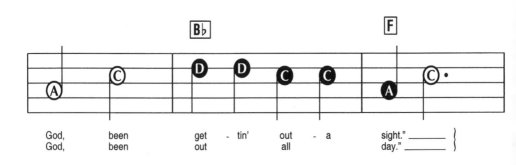

God,   been   get - tin'   out - a   sight." _____
God,   been   out   all   day." _____

Chorus

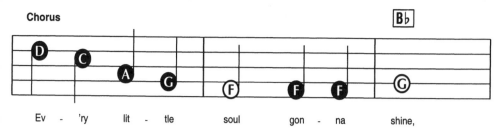

Ev - 'ry lit - tle soul gon - na shine,

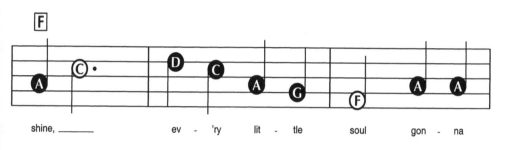

shine, _____ ev - 'ry lit - tle soul gon - na

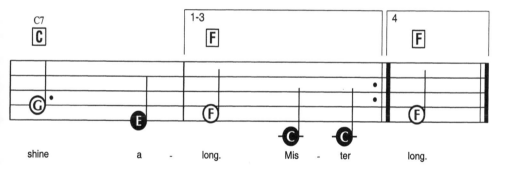

shine a - long. Mis - ter long.

Additional Lyrics

3. "Mister Rabbit, Mister Rabbit,
   your ears mighty long."
   "Yes, bless God,
   been put on wrong."
   Chorus:

4. "Mister Rabbit, Mister Rabbit,
   your ears mighty thin."
   "Yes, bless God,
   been splittin' the wind."
   Chorus:

The Monkey Song

Registration 9
Rhythm: Fox Trot

Traditional

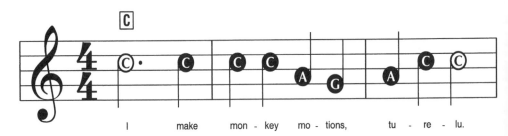

I make mon - key mo - tions, tu - re - lu.

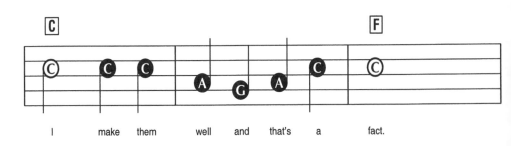

I make mon - key mo - tions, tu - re - lu.

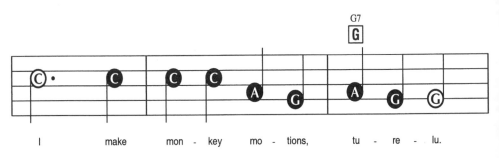

I make them well and that's a fact.

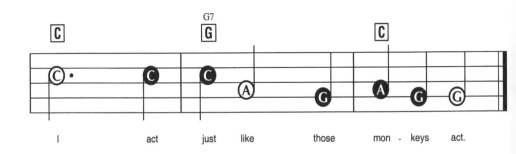

I act just like those mon - keys act.

The Muffin Man

Registration 4
Rhythm: March or Polka

Traditional

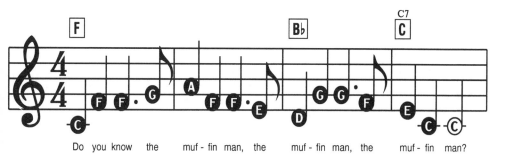

Do you know the muf - fin man, the muf - fin man, the muf - fin man?

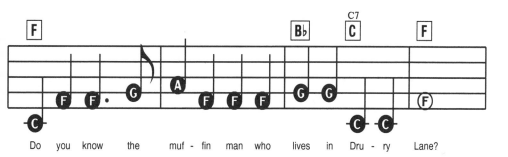

Do you know the muf - fin man who lives in Dru - ry Lane?

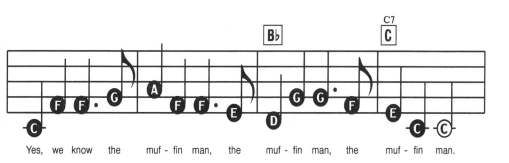

Yes, we know the muf - fin man, the muf - fin man, the muf - fin man.

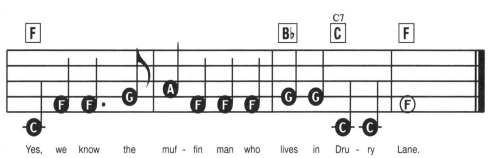

Yes, we know the muf - fin man who lives in Dru - ry Lane.

The Mulberry Bush

Registration 5
Rhythm: Waltz

Traditional

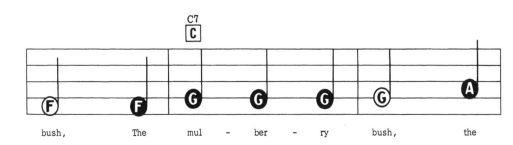

Here we go round the mul - ber - ry

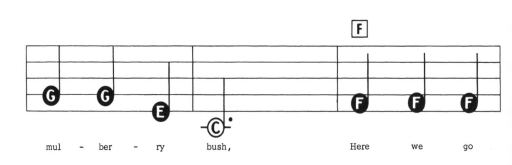

bush, The mul - ber - ry bush, the

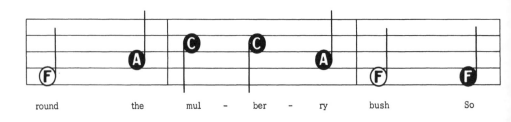

mul - ber - ry bush, Here we go

round the mul - ber - ry bush So

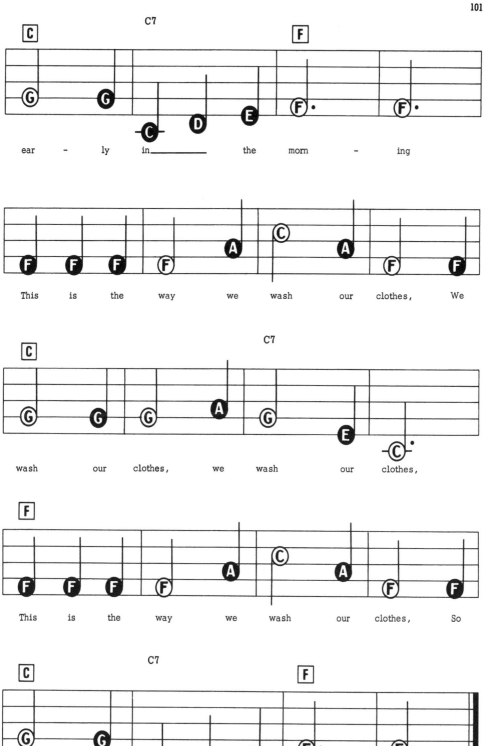

My Bonnie Lies Over the Ocean

Registration 3
Rhythm: Waltz

Traditional

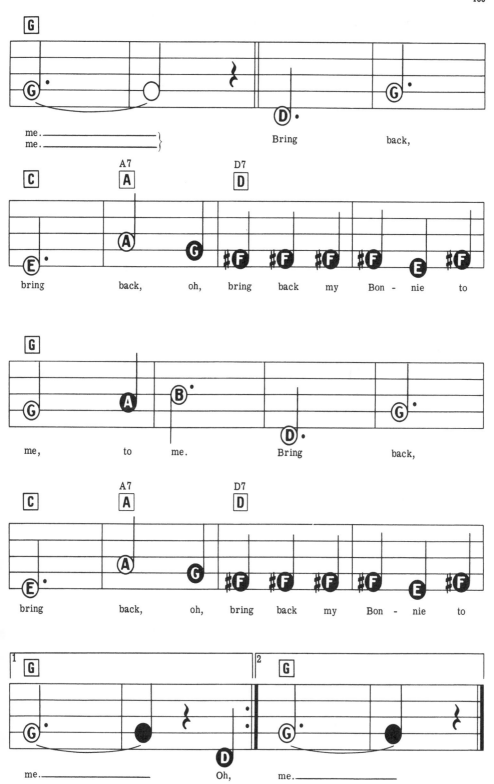

My Country, 'Tis of Thee
(America)

Registration 2
Rhythm: Waltz

Words by Samuel Francis Smith
Music from *Thesaurus Musicus*

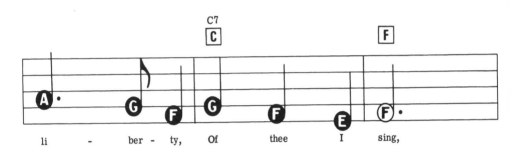

My coun - try 'tis of thee, Sweet land of

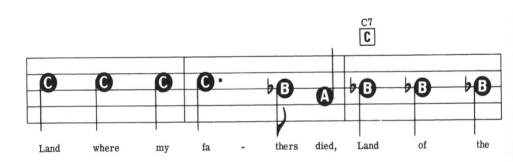

li - ber - ty, Of thee I sing,

Land where my fa - thers died, Land of the

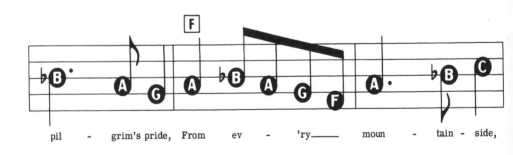

pil - grim's pride, From ev - 'ry____ moun - tain - side,

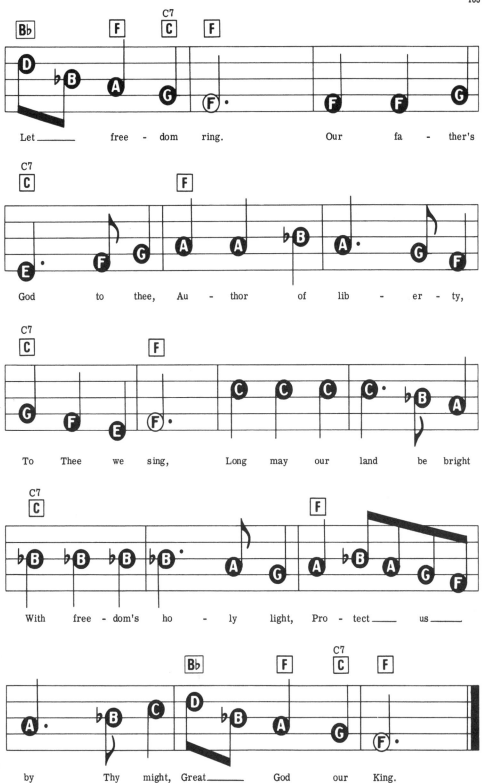

Oats, Peas, Beans and Barley Grow

Registration 5
Rhythm: Waltz

Traditional

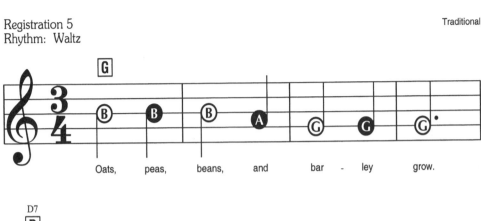

Oats, peas, beans, and bar - ley grow.

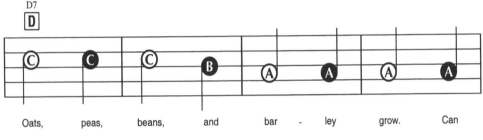

Oats, peas, beans, and bar - ley grow. Can

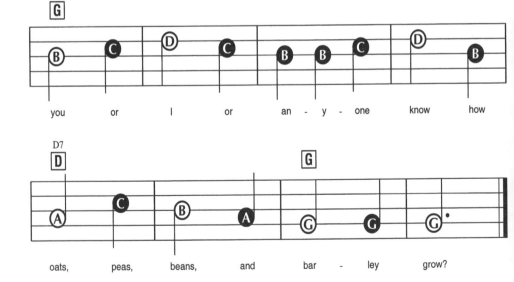

you or I or an - y - one know how

oats, peas, beans, and bar - ley grow?

Oh Where, Oh Where Has My Little Dog Gone

Registration 5
Rhythm: Waltz

Words by Sep. Winner
Traditional Melody

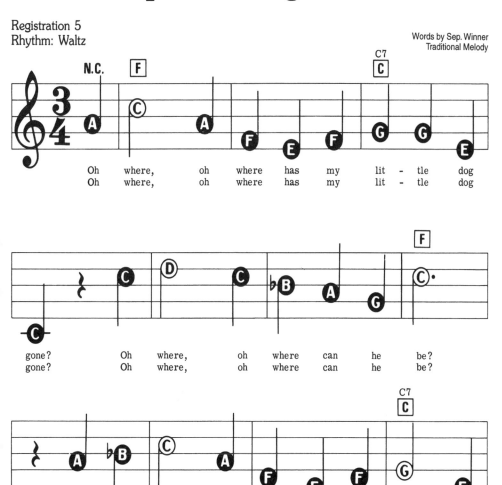

Oh where, oh where has my lit - tle dog
Oh where, oh where has my lit - tle dog

gone? Oh where, oh where can he be?
gone? Oh where, oh where can he be?

With his hair so short and his tail so
If you see him an - y - where, won't you

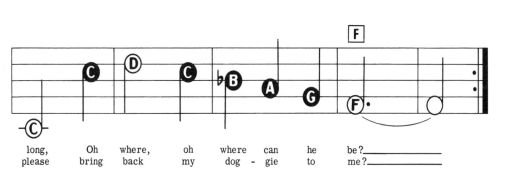

long, Oh where, oh where can he be?
please bring back my dog - gie to me?

Oh! Susanna

Registration 3
Rhythm: Fox Trot

Words and Music by
Stephen C. Foster

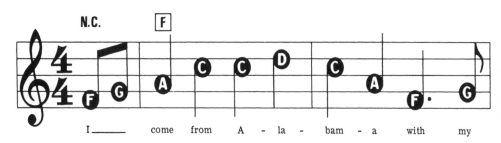

I___ come from A - la - bam - a with my

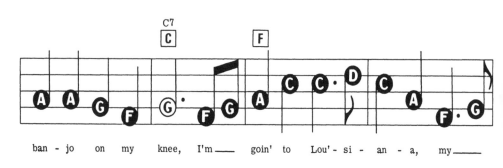

ban - jo on my knee, I'm__ goin' to Lou' - si - an - a, my__

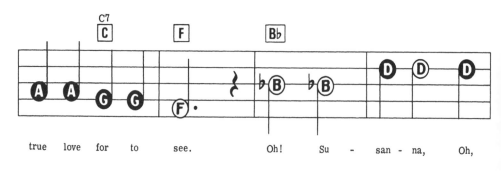

true love for to see. Oh! Su - san - na, Oh,

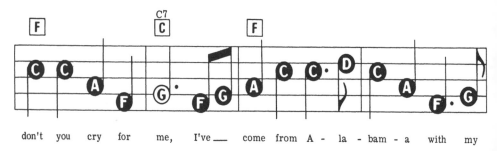

don't you cry for me, I've__ come from A - la - bam - a with my

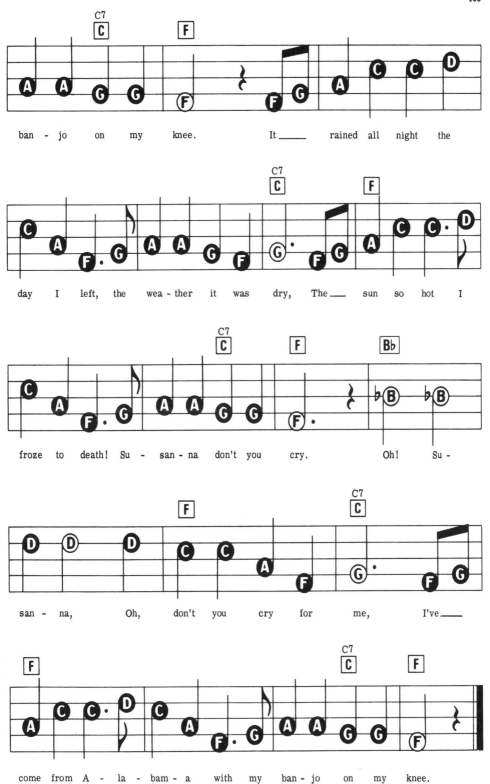

The Old Gray Mare

Registration 8
Rhythm: March

Words and Music by
J. Warner

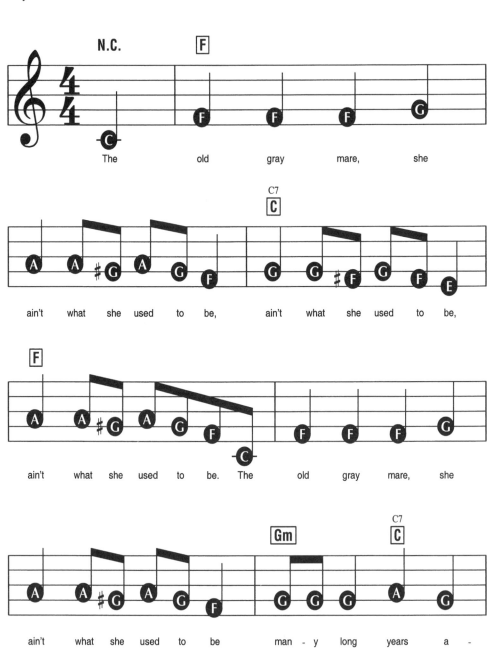

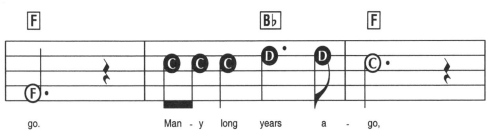

go.　　　　　　Man - y　long　years　a - go,

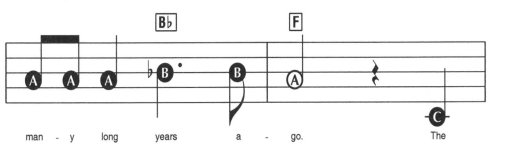

man - y　long　years　a - go.　　　　　The

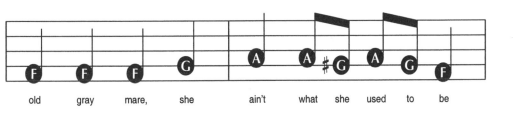

old　gray　mare,　she　ain't　what　she　used　to　be

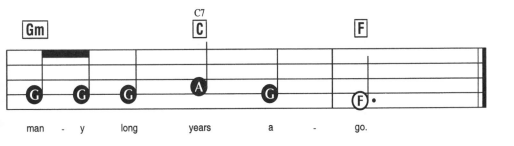

man - y　long　years　a - go.

Old King Cole

Registration 4
Rhythm: Fox Trot

Traditional

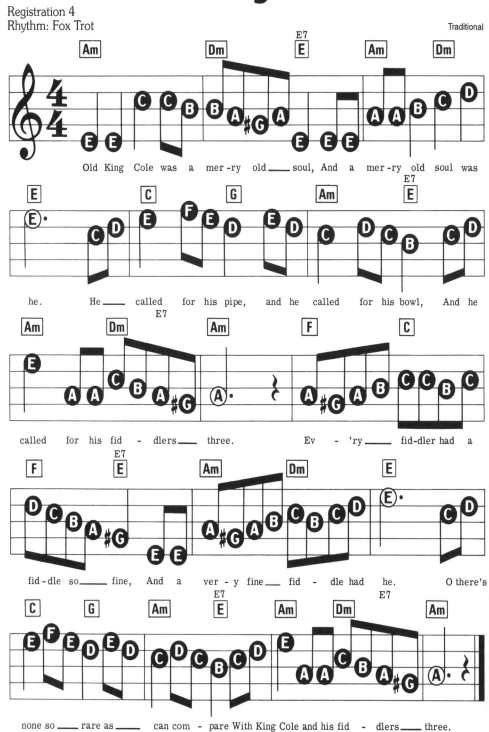

Old MacDonald

Registration 5
Rhythm: Fox Trot or Swing

Traditional Children's Song

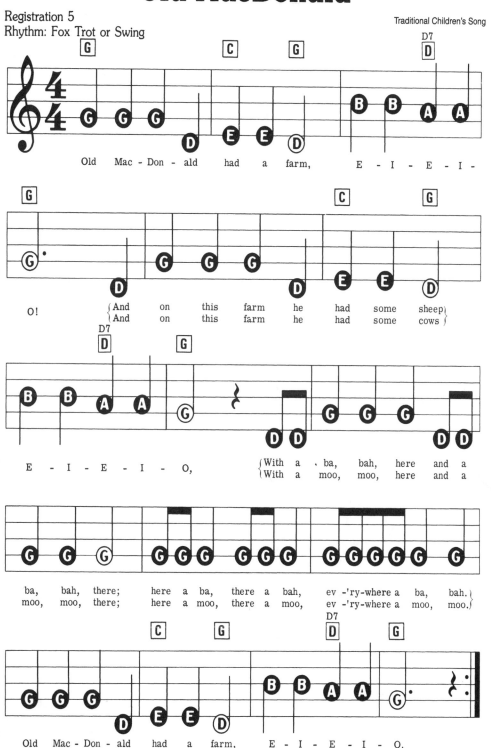

On Top of Old Smoky

Registration 1
Rhythm: Waltz

Kentucky Mountain Folksong

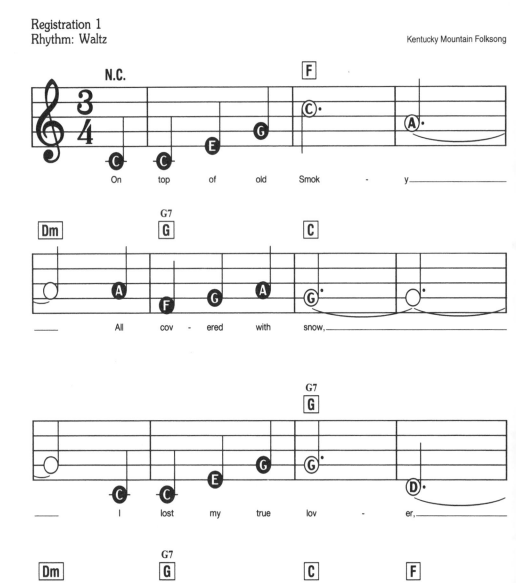

On top of old Smok - y

All cov - ered with snow,

I lost my true lov - er,

Come court - in' too slow.

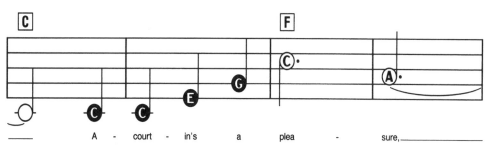

A - court - in's a plea - sure,

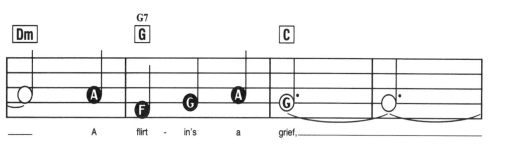

A flirt - in's a grief,

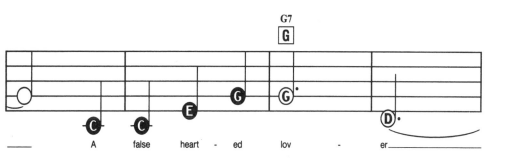

A false heart - ed lov - er

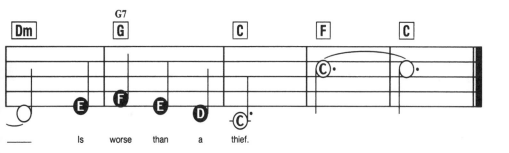

Is worse than a thief.

Over the River and Through the Woods

Registration 8
Rhythm: 6/8 March

Traditional

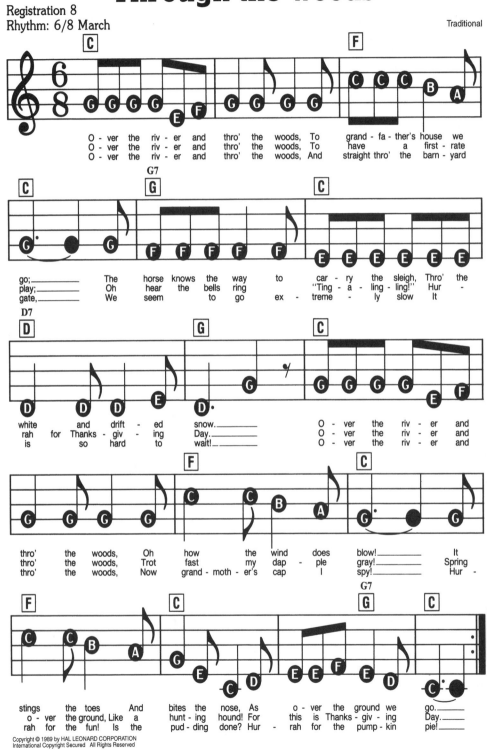

O - ver the riv - er and thro' the woods, To grand - fa - ther's house we
O - ver the riv - er and thro' the woods, To have a first - rate
O - ver the riv - er and thro' the woods, And straight thro' the barn - yard

go;_____ The horse knows the way to car - ry the sleigh, Thro' the
play;_____ Oh hear the bells ring "Ting - a - ling - ling!" Hur -
gate,_____ We seem to go ex - treme - ly slow It

white and drift - ed snow._____ O - ver the riv - er and
rah for Thanks - giv - ing Day._____ O - ver the riv - er and
is so hard to wait!_____ O - ver the riv - er and

thro' the woods, Oh how the wind does blow!_____ It
thro' the woods, Trot fast my dap - ple gray!_____ Spring
thro' the woods, Now grand - moth - er's cap I spy!_____ Hur -

stings the toes And bites the nose, As o - ver the ground we go._____
o - ver the ground, Like a hunt - ing hound! For this is Thanks - giv - ing Day._____
rah for the fun! Is the pud - ding done? Hur - rah for the pump - kin pie!_____

The Paw Paw Patch

Registration 1
Rhythm: Polka, March or Rock

Traditional

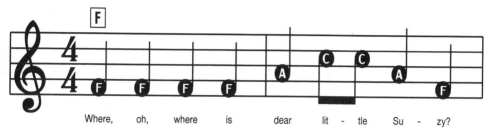

Where, oh, where is dear lit - tle Su - zy?

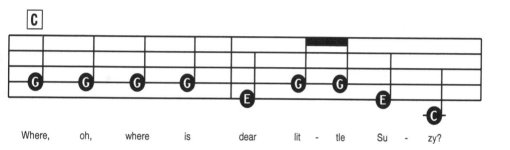

Where, oh, where is dear lit - tle Su - zy?

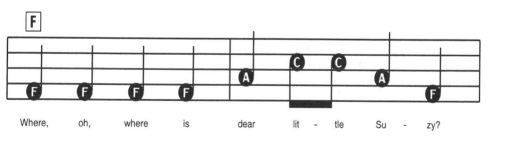

Where, oh, where is dear lit - tle Su - zy?

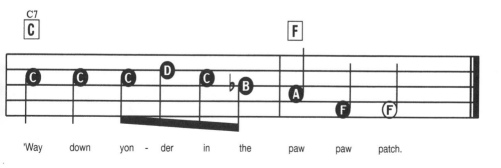

'Way down yon - der in the paw paw patch.

Peanut Sat on a Railroad Track

Registration 8
Rhythm: Polka or March

Traditional

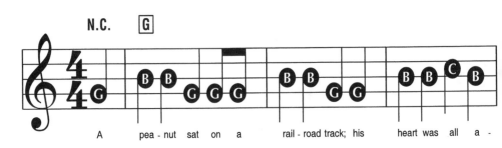

A pea-nut sat on a rail-road track; his heart was all a-

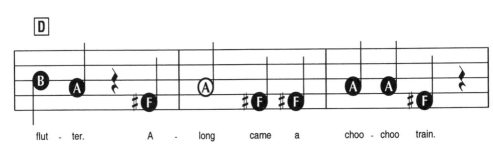

flut - ter. A - long came a choo - choo train.

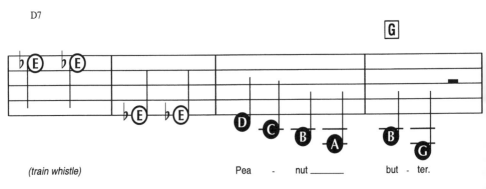

(train whistle) Pea - nut _____ but - ter.

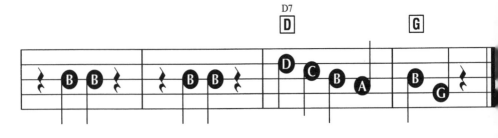

Pease Porridge Hot

Registration 8
Rhythm: Fox Trot

Traditional

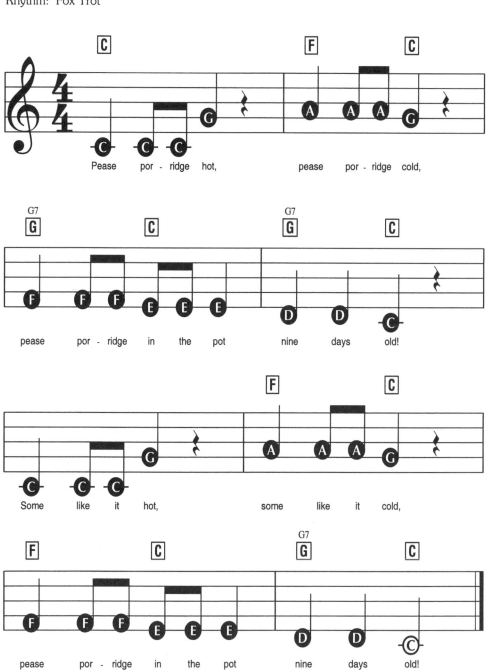

Peter, Peter, Pumpkin Eater

Registration 7
Rhythm: Polka or March

Traditional

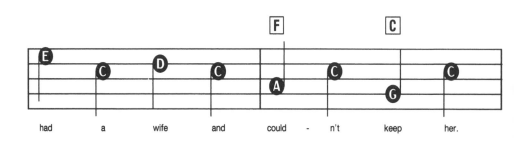

Pe - ter, Pe - ter, pump - kin eat - er,

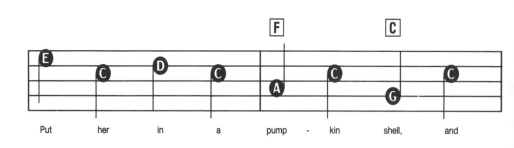

had a wife and could - n't keep her.

Put her in a pump - kin shell, and

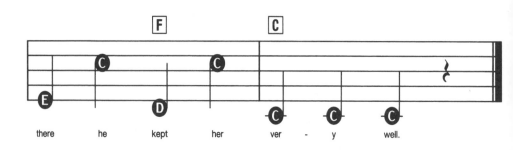

there he kept her ver - y well.

Polly Put the Kettle On

Registration 4
Rhythm: Fox Trot or Swing

Traditional

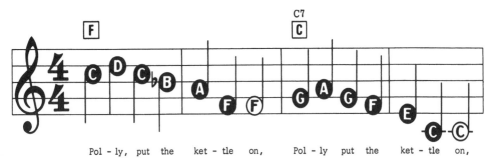

Pol - ly, put the ket - tle on, Pol - ly put the ket - tle on,

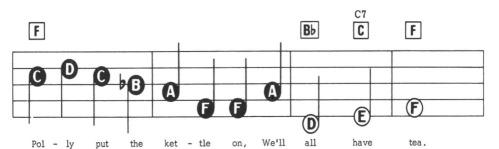

Pol - ly put the ket - tle on, We'll all have tea.

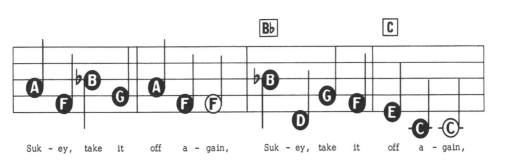

Suk - ey, take it off a - gain, Suk - ey, take it off a - gain,

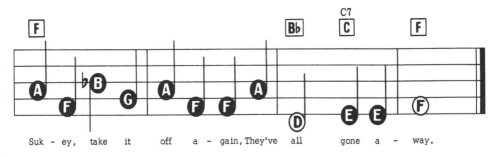

Suk - ey, take it off a - gain, They've all gone a - way.

Pop Goes the Weasel

Registration 5
Rhythm: Waltz

Traditional

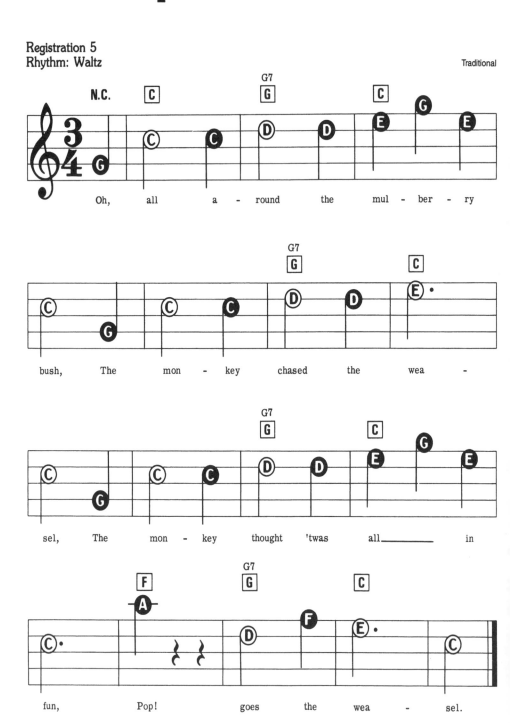

Oh, all a - round the mul - ber - ry

bush, The mon - key chased the wea -

sel, The mon - key thought 'twas all_____ in

fun, Pop! goes the wea - sel.

Rock-A-Bye, Baby

Registration 3
Rhythm: Waltz

Traditional

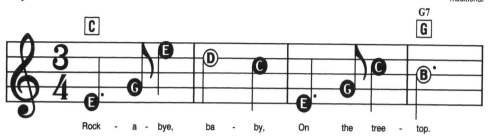

Rock - a - bye, ba - by, On the tree - top.

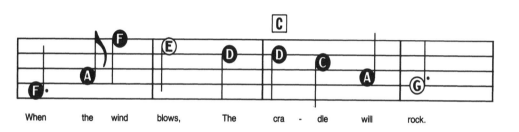

When the wind blows, The cra - dle will rock.

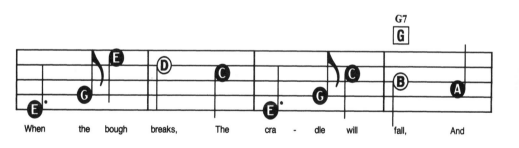

When the bough breaks, The cra - dle will fall, And

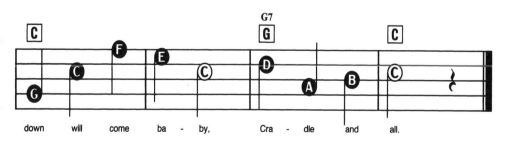

down will come ba - by, Cra - dle and all.

Row, Row, Row Your Boat

Registration 5
Rhythm: Waltz

Traditional

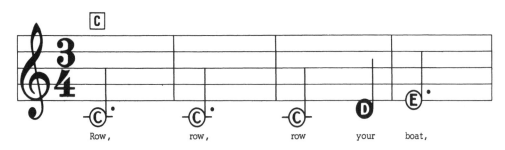

Row, row, row your boat,

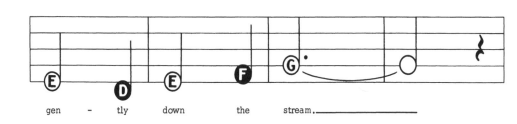

gen - tly down the stream.

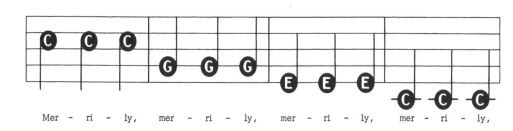

Mer - ri - ly, mer - ri - ly, mer - ri - ly, mer - ri - ly,

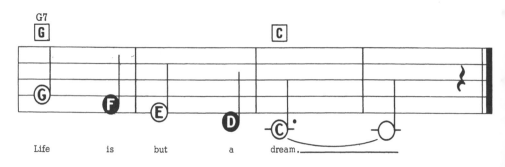

Life is but a dream.

Simple Simon

Registration 9
Rhythm: Fox Trot

Traditional

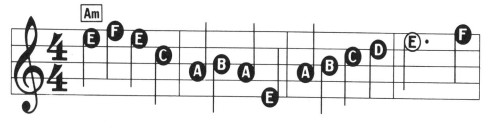

Sim - ple Si - mon met a pie - man go - ing to the fair, Says

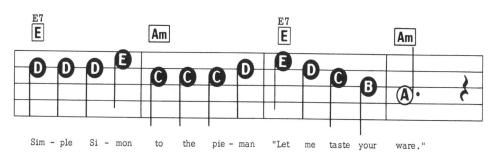

Sim - ple Si - mon to the pie - man "Let me taste your ware."

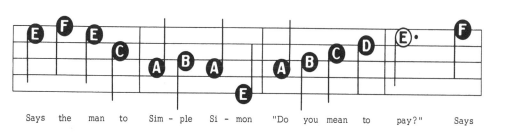

Says the man to Sim - ple Si - mon "Do you mean to pay?" Says

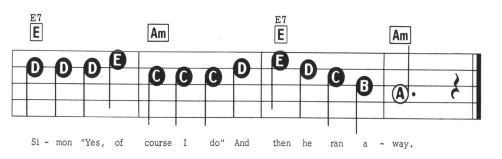

Si - mon "Yes, of course I do" And then he ran a - way.

She'll Be Comin' 'Round the Mountain

Registration 8
Rhythm: Bluegrass or Fox Trot

Traditional

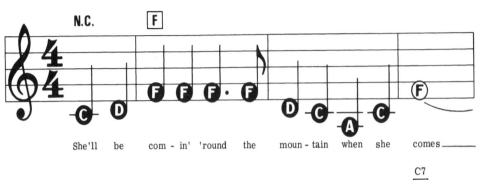

She'll be com - in' 'round the moun - tain when she comes___

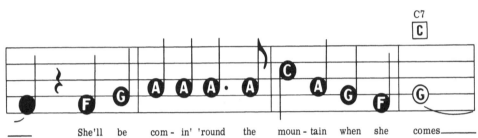

She'll be com - in' 'round the moun - tain when she comes___

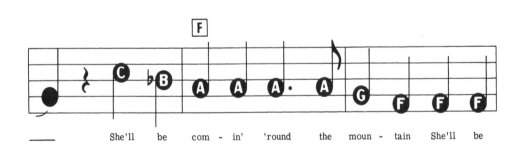

She'll be com - in' 'round the moun - tain She'll be

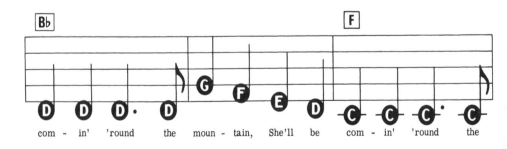

com - in' 'round the moun - tain, She'll be com - in' 'round the

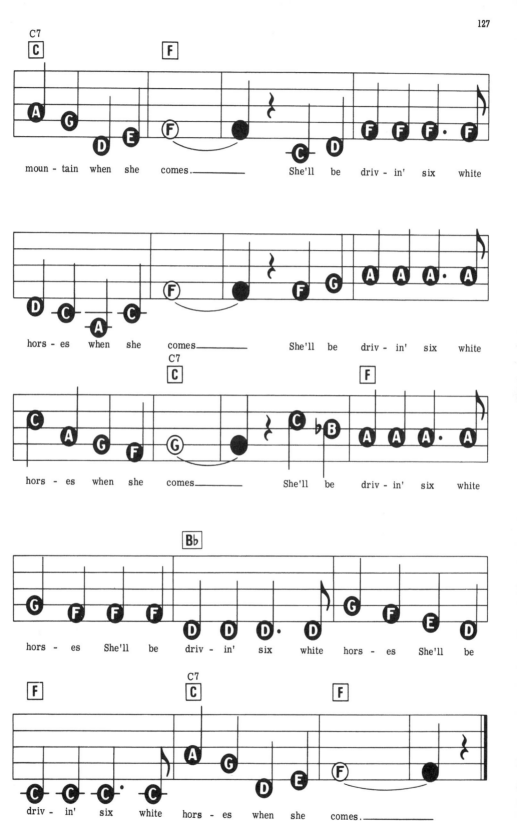

Shoo Fly, Don't Bother Me

Registration 9
Rhythm: Country or Fox Trot

Words by Billy Reeves
Music by Frank Campbell

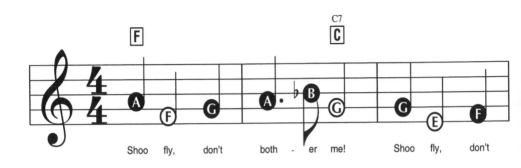

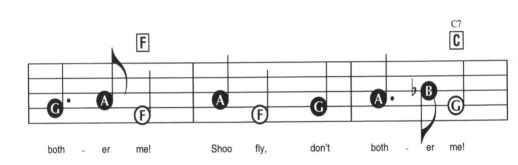

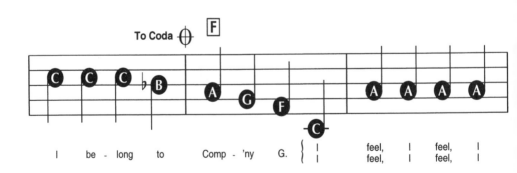

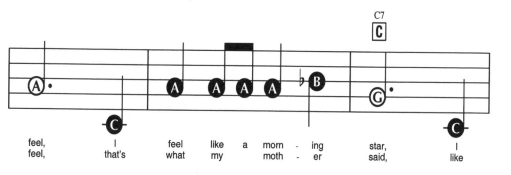

feel, | feel like a morn - ing star, |
feel, that's what my moth - er said, like

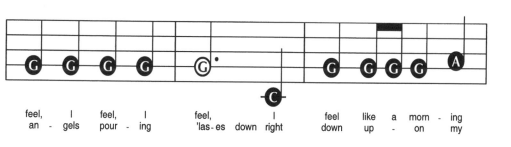

feel, | feel, | feel, | feel like a morn - ing
an - gels pour - ing 'las-es down right down up - on my

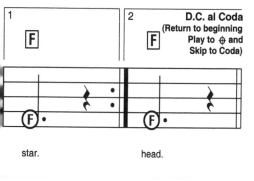

D.C. al Coda
(Return to beginning
Play to ⊕ and
Skip to Coda)

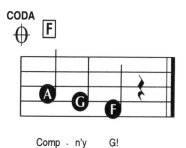

star. head.

Comp - n'y G!

Simple Gifts

Registration 8
Rhythm: Fox Trot

Traditional Shaker Hymn

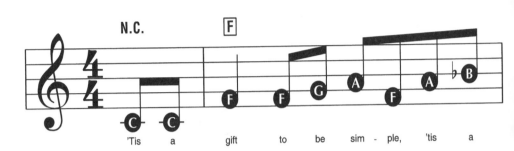

'Tis a gift to be sim - ple, 'tis a

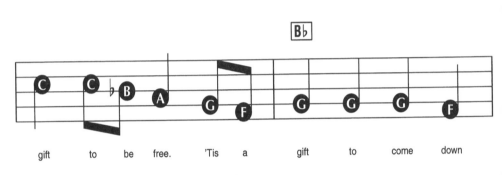

gift to be free. 'Tis a gift to come down

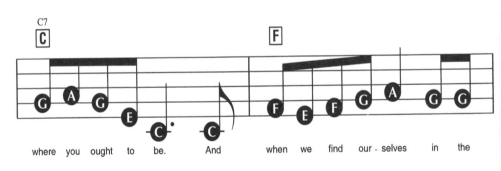

where you ought to be. And when we find our - selves in the

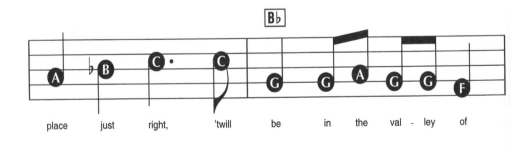

place just right, 'twill be in the val - ley of

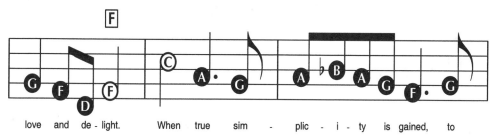

love and de-light. When true sim - plic - i - ty is gained, to

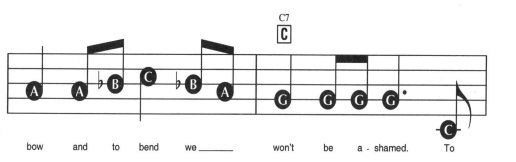

bow and to bend we _____ won't be a - shamed. To

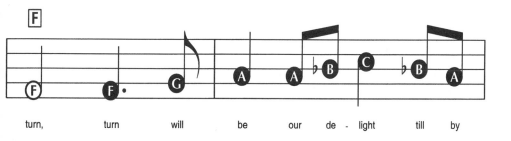

turn, turn will be our de - light till by

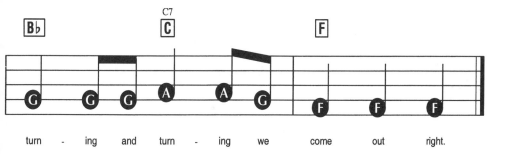

turn - ing and turn - ing we come out right.

Skip to My Lou

Registration 10
Rhythm: Fox Trot

Traditional

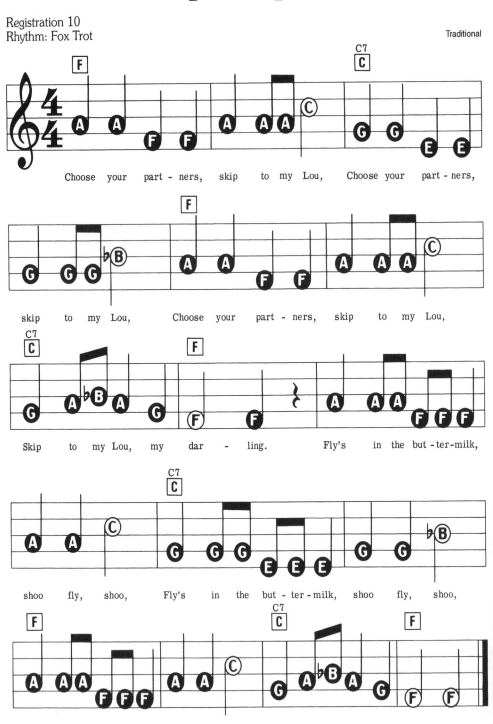

Sweet Betsy from Pike

Registration 5
Rhythm: Waltz

American Folksong

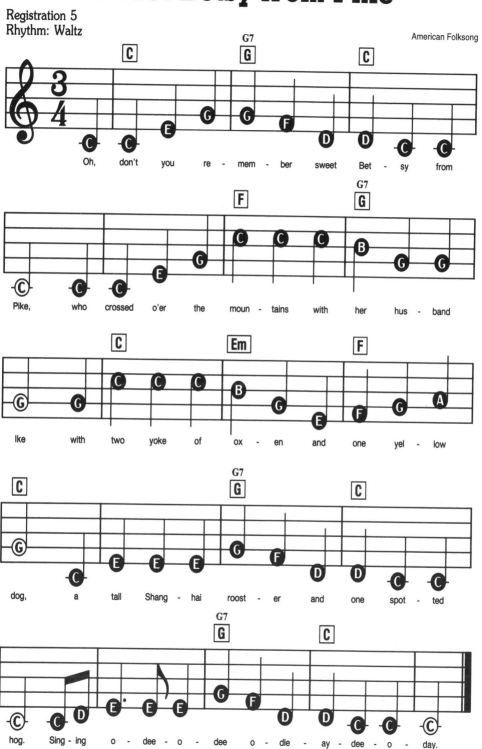

Oh, don't you re - mem - ber sweet Bet - sy from Pike, who crossed o'er the moun - tains with her hus - band Ike with two yoke of ox - en and one yel - low dog, a tall Shang - hai roost - er and one spot - ted hog. Sing - ing o - dee - o - dee o - dle - ay - dee - o - day.

Take Me Out to the Ball Game

Registration 3
Rhythm: Waltz

Words by Jack Norworth
Music by Albert von Tilzer

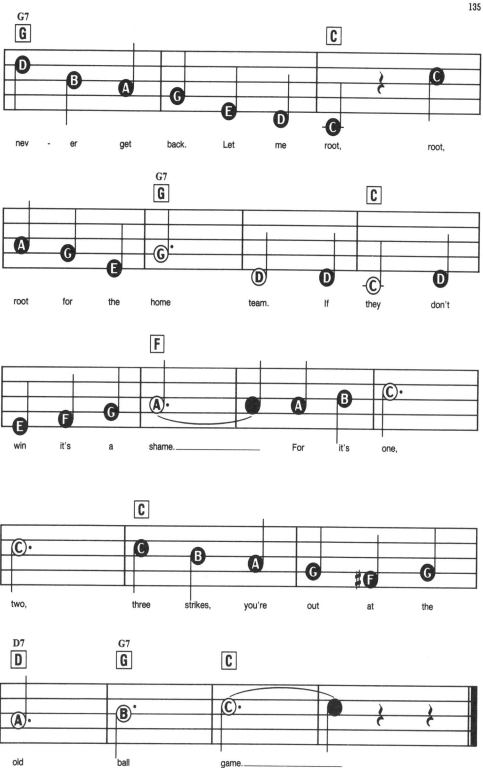

There Was an Old Woman Who Lived in a Shoe

Registration 4
Rhythm: Rock or 8 Beat

Traditional

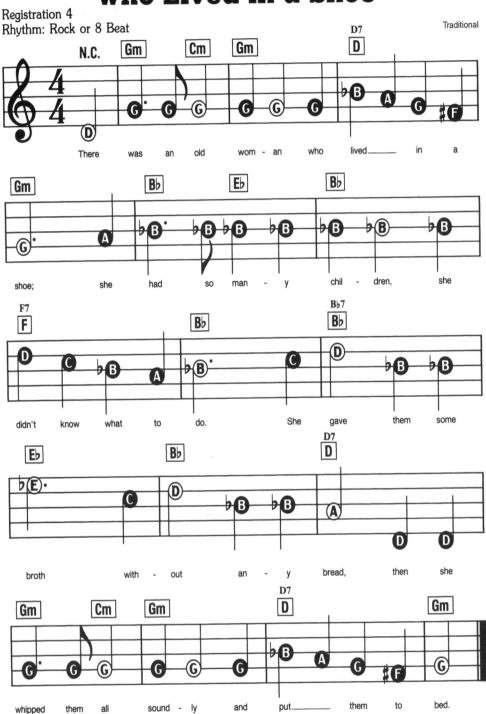

There was an old wom-an who lived____ in a shoe; she had so man-y chil-dren, she didn't know what to do. She gave them some broth with-out an-y bread, then she whipped them all sound-ly and put____ them to bed.

There's a Hole in the Bucket

Registration 10
Rhythm: Waltz

Traditional

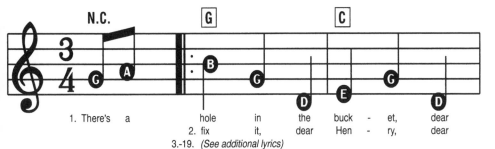

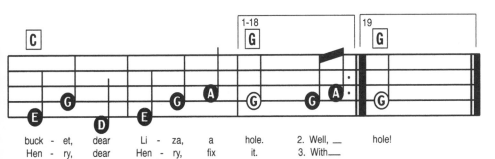

1. There's a hole in the buck - et, dear
2. fix it, dear Hen - ry, dear
3.-19. *(See additional lyrics)*

Li - za, dear Li - za. There's a hole in the
Hen - ry, dear Hen - ry. Well, ___ fix it, dear

buck - et, dear Li - za, a hole. 2. Well, ___ hole!
Hen - ry, dear Hen - ry, fix it. 3. With___

Additional Lyrics

3. With what shall I fix it, dear Liza, *etc.*
4. With a straw, dear Henry, *etc.*
5. But the straw is too long, dear Liza, *etc.*
6. Then cut it, dear Henry, *etc.*
7. With what shall I cut it, dear Liza, *etc.*
8. With a knife, dear Henry, *etc.*
9. But the knife is too dull, dear Liza, *etc.*
10. Then sharpen it, dear Henry, *etc.*
11. With what shall I sharpen it, dear Liza, *etc.*
12. With a stone, dear Henry, *etc.*
13. But the stone is too dry, dear Liza, *etc.*
14. Then wet it, dear Henry, *etc.*
15. With what shall I wet it, dear Liza, *etc.*
16. With water, dear Henry, *etc.*
17. In what shall I carry it, dear Liza, *etc.*
18. In a bucket, dear Henry, *etc.*
19. There's a hole in the bucket, dear Liza, *etc.*

There's a Hole
in the Bottom of the Sea

Registration 1
Rhythm: Shuffle or Swing

Traditional

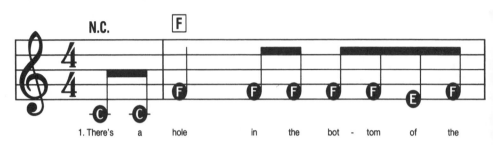

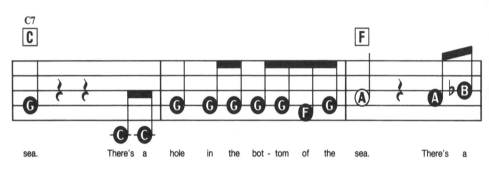

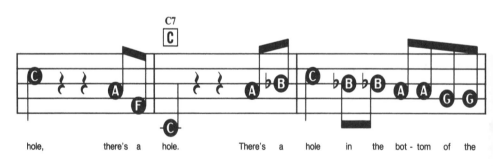

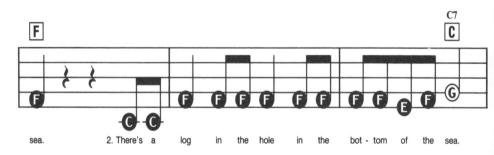

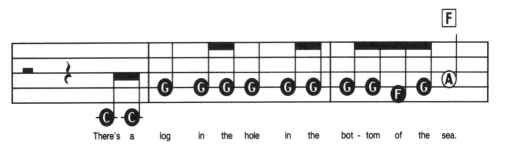

There's a log in the hole in the bot - tom of the sea.

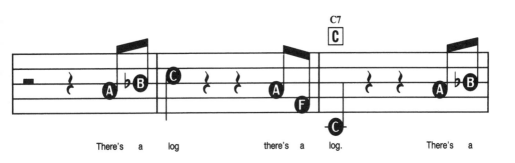

There's a log there's a log. There's a

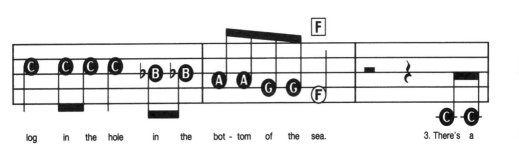

log in the hole in the bot - tom of the sea. 3. There's a

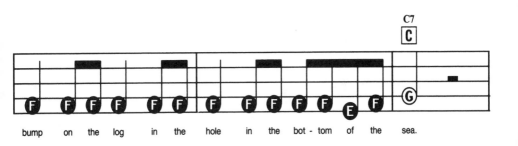

bump on the log in the hole in the bot - tom of the sea.

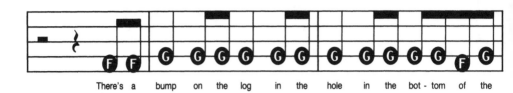

There's a bump on the log in the hole in the bot - tom of the

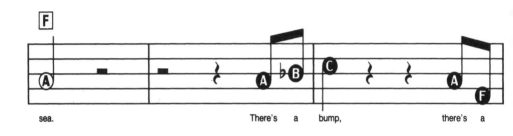

sea.   There's a bump,   there's a

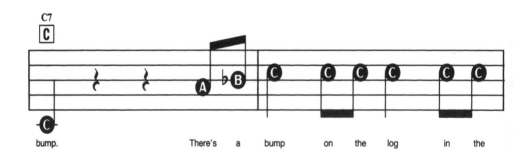

bump.   There's a bump on the log in the

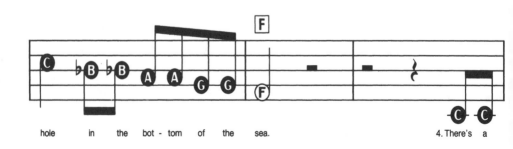

hole in the bot - tom of the sea.   4. There's a

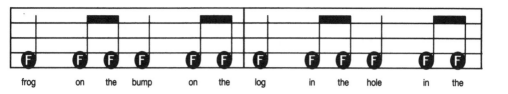

frog · on · the · bump · on · the · log · in · the · hole · in · the

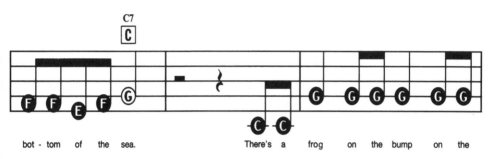

bot - tom · of · the · sea. · There's · a · frog · on · the · bump · on · the

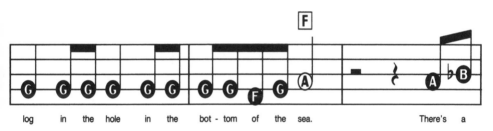

log · in · the · hole · in · the · bot - tom · of · the · sea. · There's · a

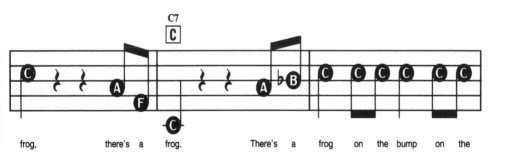

frog, · there's · a · frog. · There's · a · frog · on · the · bump · on · the

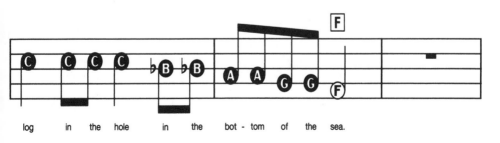

log · in · the · hole · in · the · bot - tom · of · the · sea.

142

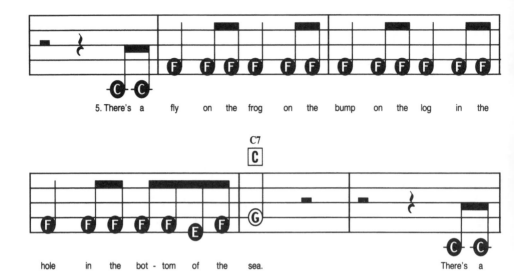

5. There's a fly on the frog on the bump on the log in the

C7

hole in the bot - tom of the sea. There's a

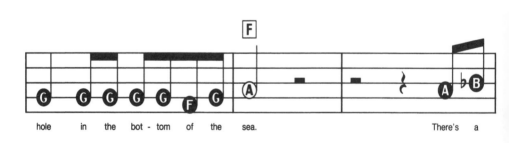

fly on the frog on the bump on the log in the

F

hole in the bot - tom of the sea. There's a

C7

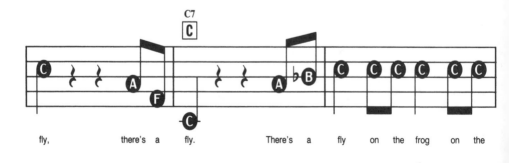

fly, there's a fly. There's a fly on the frog on the

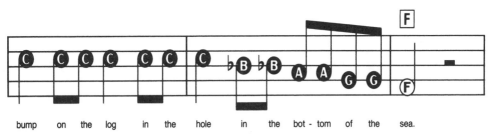

bump   on   the   log   in   the   hole   in   the   bot - tom   of   the   sea.

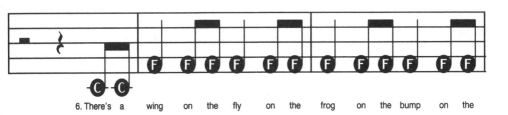

6. There's a   wing   on   the   fly   on   the   frog   on   the   bump   on   the

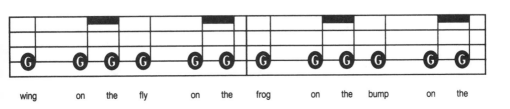

log   in   the   hole   in   the   bot - tom   of   the   sea.   There's a

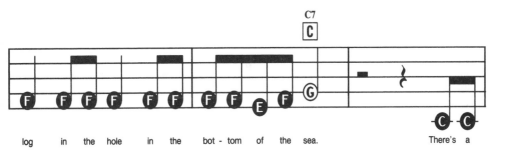

wing   on   the   fly   on   the   frog   on   the   bump   on   the

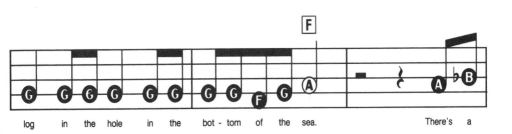

log   in   the   hole   in   the   bot - tom   of   the   sea.   There's   a

144

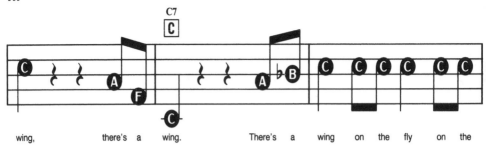

wing,   there's a   wing.   There's a   wing   on   the   fly   on   the

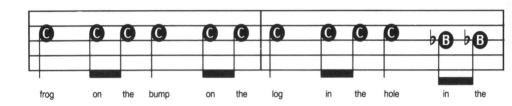

frog   on   the   bump   on   the   log   in   the   hole   in   the

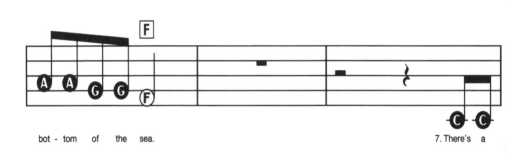

bot - tom   of   the   sea.   7. There's   a

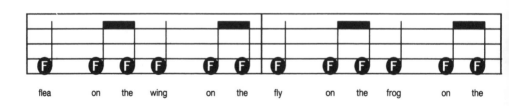

flea   on   the   wing   on   the   fly   on   the   frog   on   the

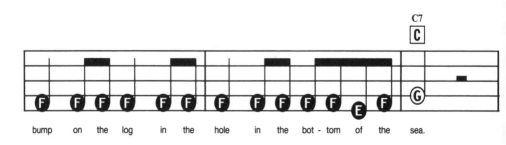

bump   on   the   log   in   the   hole   in   the   bot - tom   of   the   sea.

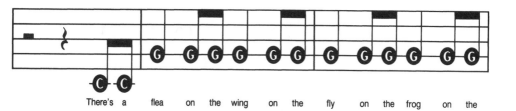

There's a flea on the wing on the fly on the frog on the

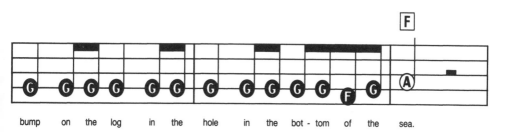

bump on the log in the hole in the bot - tom of the sea.

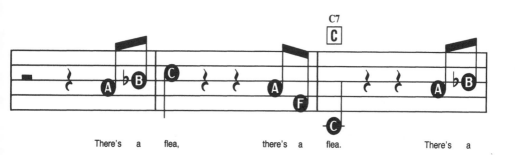

There's a flea, there's a flea. There's a

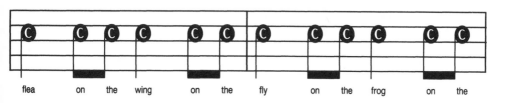

flea on the wing on the fly on the frog on the

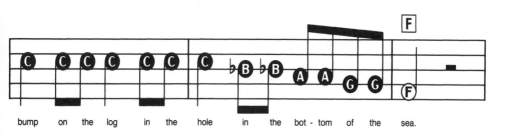

bump on the log in the hole in the bot - tom of the sea.

8. There's an eye on the flea on the wing on the fly on the

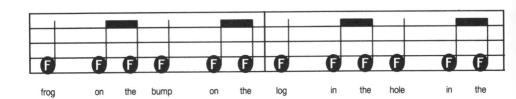

frog on the bump on the log in the hole in the

C7

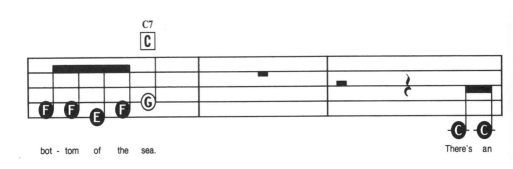

bot - tom of the sea.   There's an

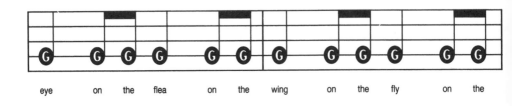

eye on the flea on the wing on the fly on the

F

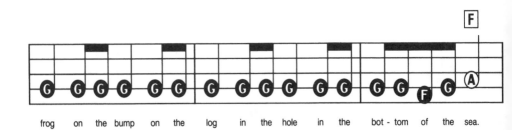

frog on the bump on the log in the hole in the bot - tom of the sea.

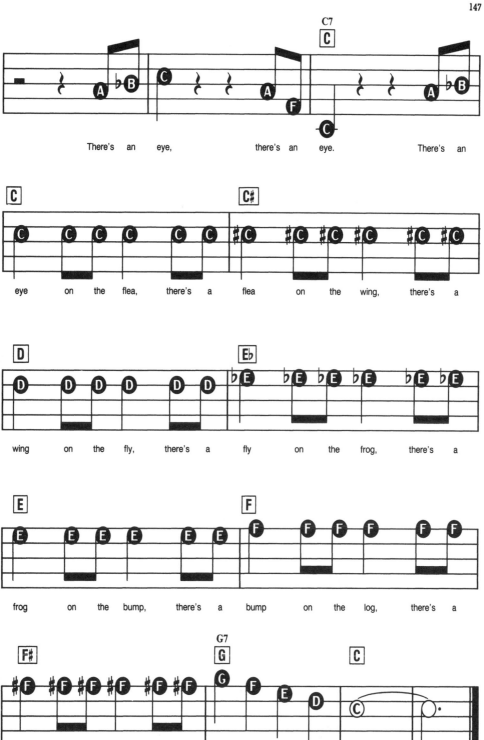

This Little Light of Mine

Registration 4
Rhythm: Fox Trot or Swing

African-American Spiritual

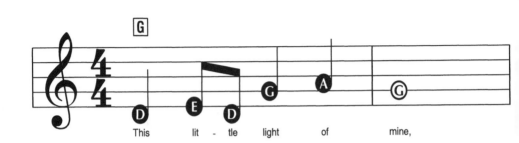

This lit - tle light of mine,

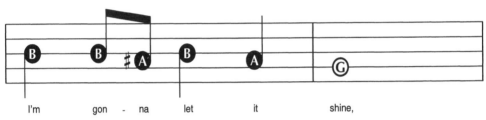

I'm gon - na let it shine,

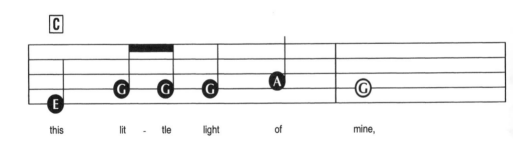

this lit - tle light of mine,

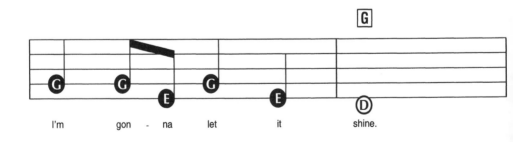

I'm gon - na let it shine.

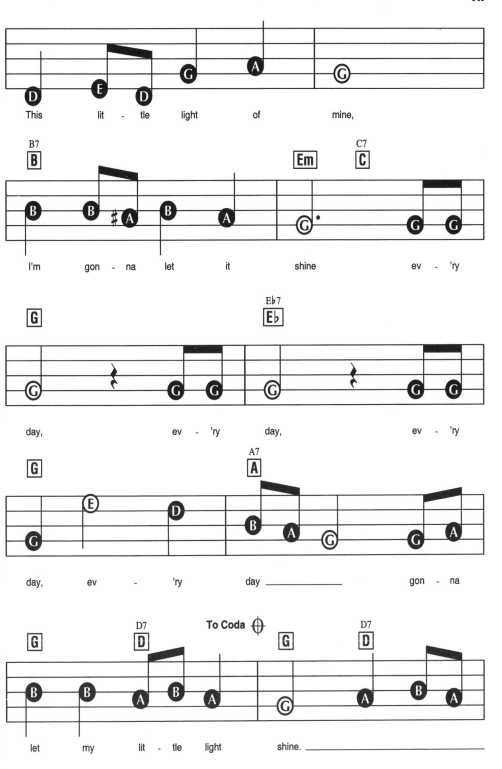

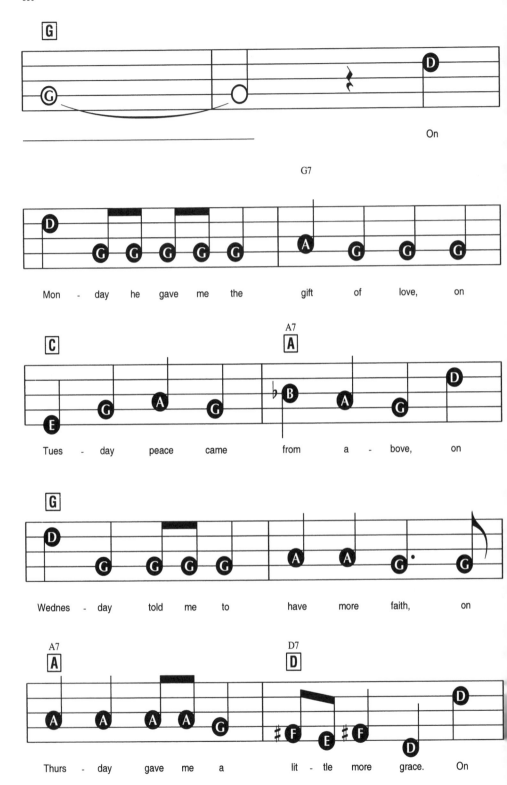

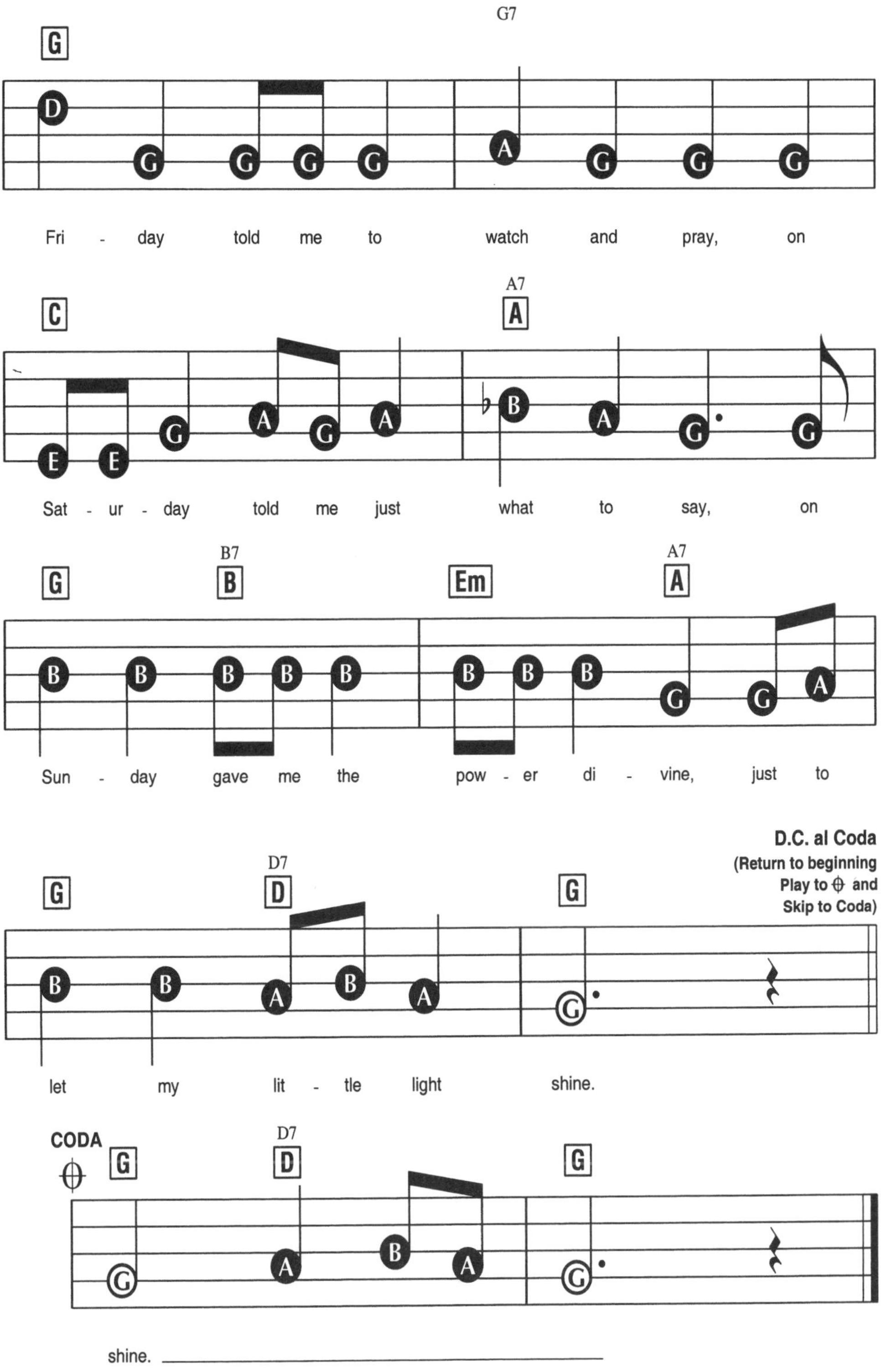

G7
G
Fri - day told me to watch and pray, on
A7
C A
Sat - ur - day told me just what to say, on
B7 A7
G B Em A
Sun - day gave me the pow - er di - vine, just to
D.C. al Coda
(Return to beginning
Play to ⊕ and
Skip to Coda)
D7
G D G
let my lit - tle light shine.
CODA
D7
G D G
shine.

This Old Man

Registration 5
Rhythm: Fox Trot

Traditional

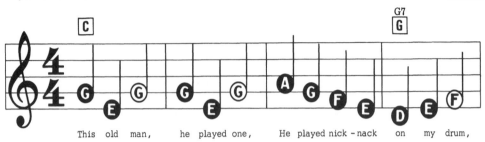

This old man, he played one, He played nick-nack on my drum,

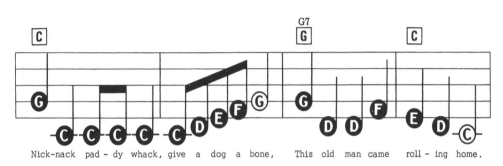

Nick-nack pad-dy whack, give a dog a bone, This old man came roll-ing home.

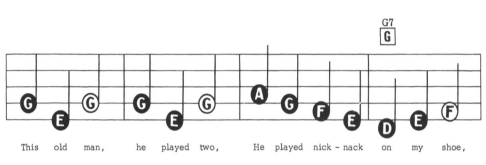

This old man, he played two, He played nick-nack on my shoe,

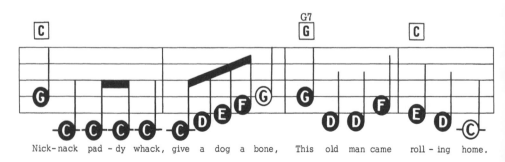

Nick-nack pad-dy whack, give a dog a bone, This old man came roll-ing home.

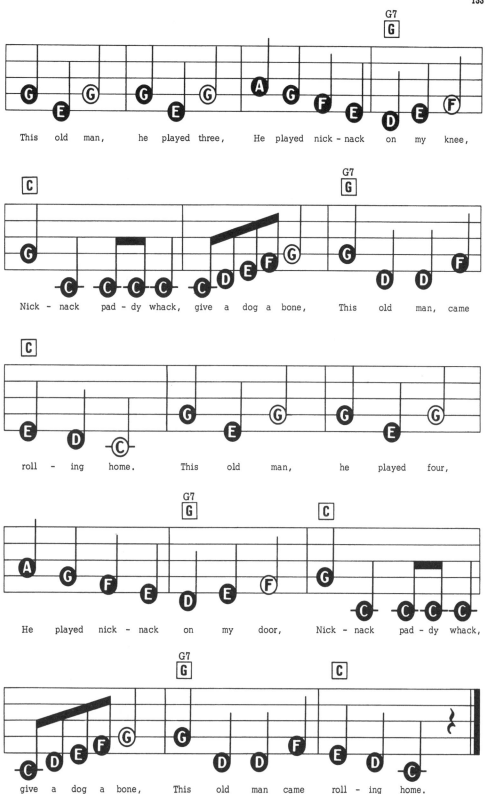

Three Blind Mice

Registration 1
Rhythm: Waltz

Traditional

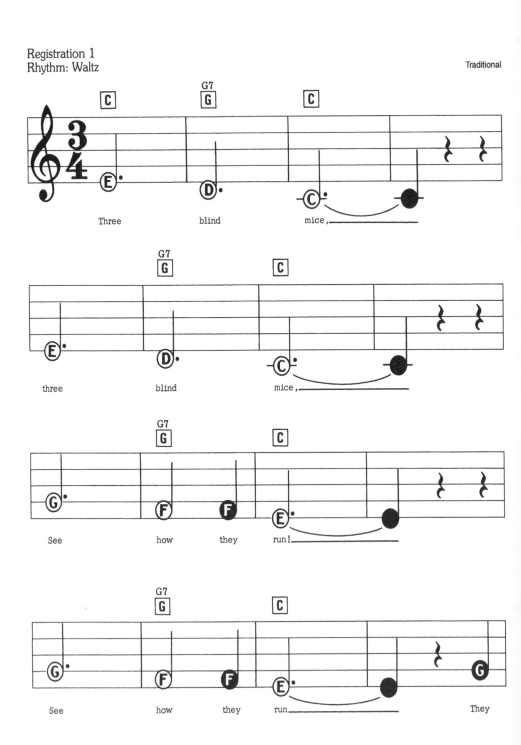

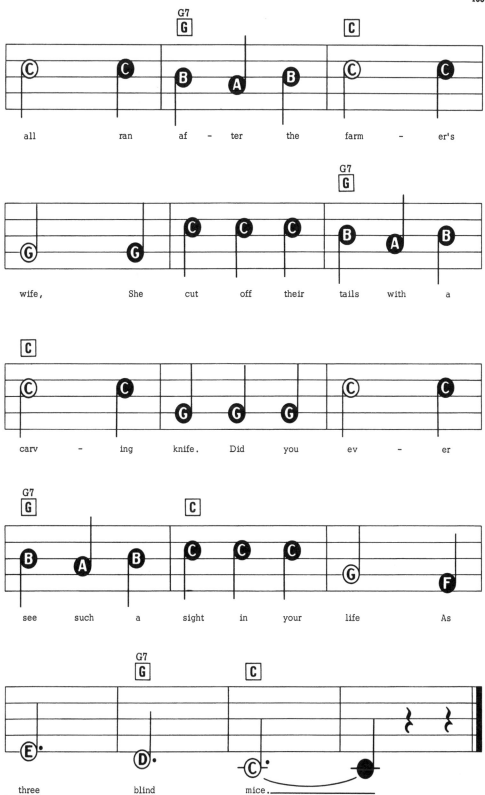

Three Little Kittens

Registration 7
Rhythm: Waltz

Traditional

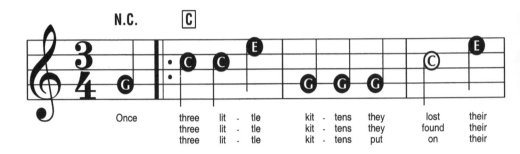

Once three lit - tle kit - tens they lost their
three lit - tle kit - tens they found their
three lit - tle kit - tens put on their

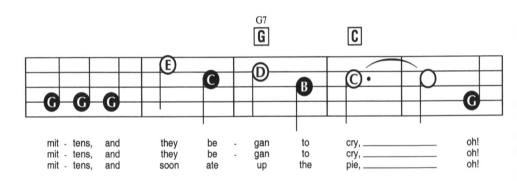

mit - tens, and they be - gan to cry, _____ oh!
mit - tens, and they be - gan to cry, _____ oh!
mit - tens, and soon ate up the pie, _____ oh!

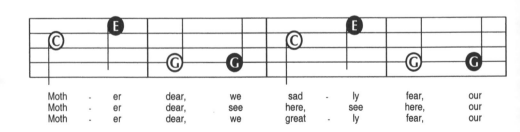

Moth - er dear, we sad - ly fear, our
Moth - er dear, see here, see here, our
Moth - er dear, we great - ly fear, our

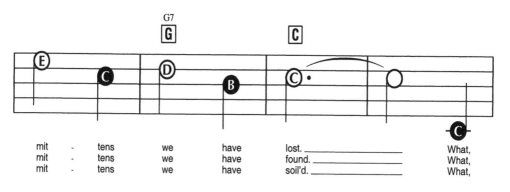

mit	-	tens	we	have	lost. _____	What,
mit	-	tens	we	have	found. _____	What,
mit	-	tens	we	have	soil'd. _____	What,

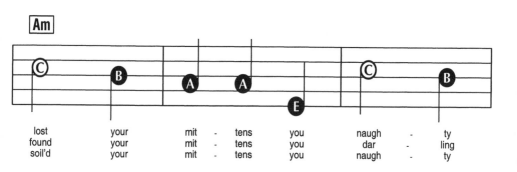

lost	your	mit	-	tens	you	naugh	-	ty
found	your	mit	-	tens	you	dar	-	ling
soil'd	your	mit	-	tens	you	naugh	-	ty

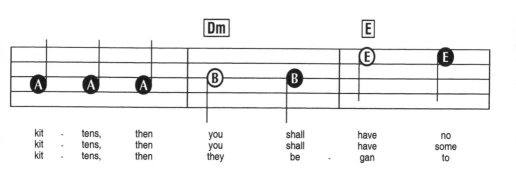

kit	-	tens,	then	you	shall	have	no
kit	-	tens,	then	you	shall	have	some
kit	-	tens,	then	they	be	-	gan	to

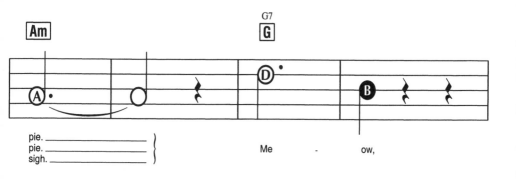

pie. _____		
pie. _____	Me	-	ow,
sigh. _____		

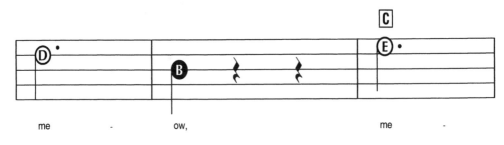

me - ow, me -

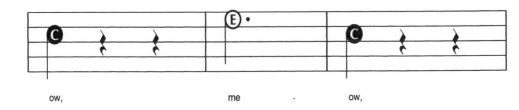

ow, me - ow,

G7

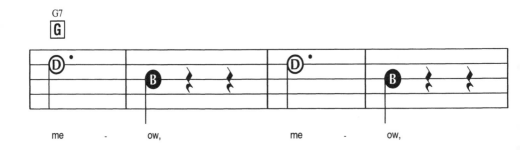

me - ow, me - ow,

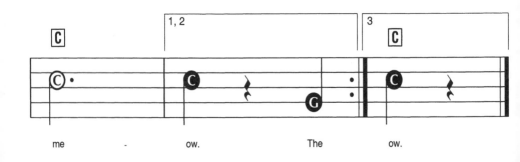

me - ow. The ow.

Tom, Tom, the Piper's Son

Registration 4
Rhythm: Fox Trot

Traditional

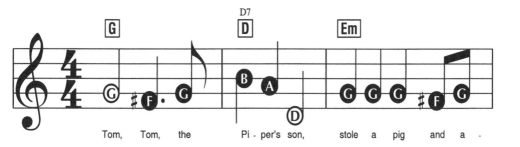

Tom, Tom, the Pi - per's son, stole a pig and a -

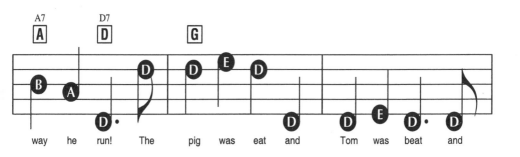

way he run! The pig was eat and Tom was beat and

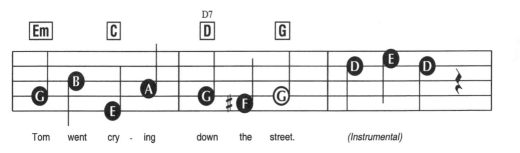

Tom went cry - ing down the street. *(Instrumental)*

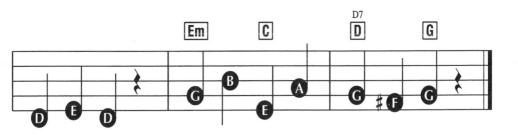

Twinkle, Twinkle Little Star

Registration 1
Rhythm: Swing

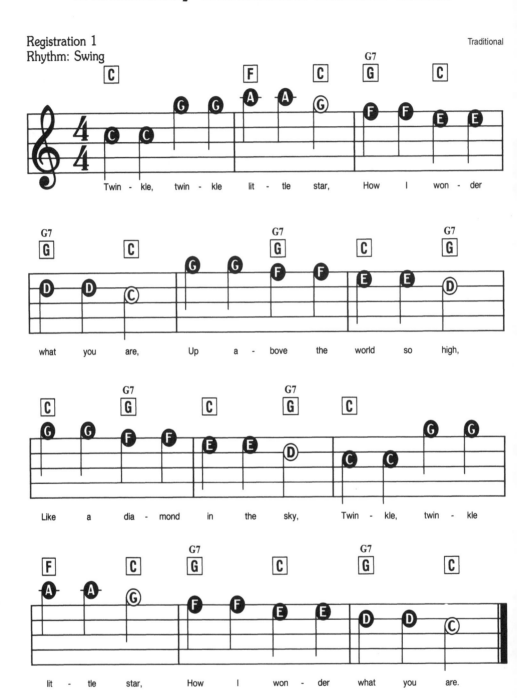

When the Saints Go Marching In

Registration 2
Rhythm: Swing

Words by Katherine E. Purvis
Music by James M. Black

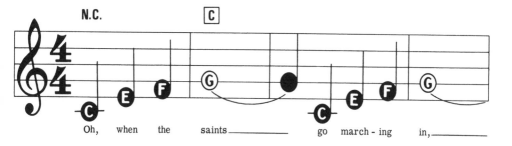

Oh, when the saints go march-ing in,

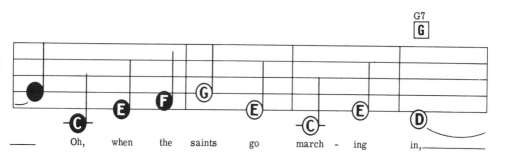

Oh, when the saints go march - ing in,

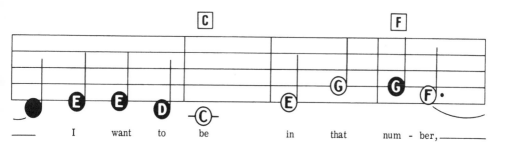

I want to be in that num - ber,

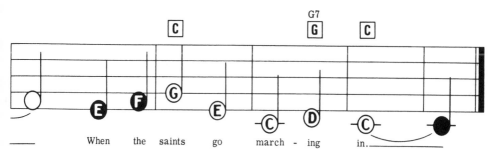

When the saints go march - ing in.

Yankee Doodle

Registration 9
Rhythm: March

Traditional

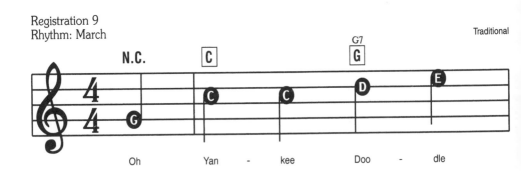

Oh   Yan - kee   Doo -   dle

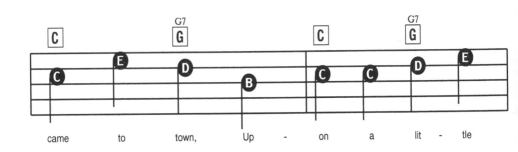

came   to   town,   Up - on   a   lit - tle

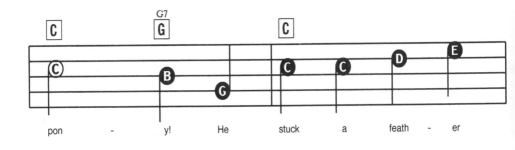

pon -   y!   He   stuck   a   feath - er

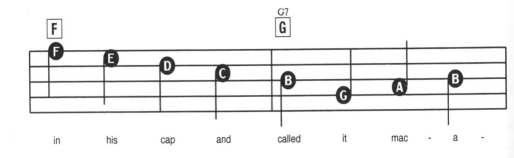

in   his   cap   and   called   it   mac - a -

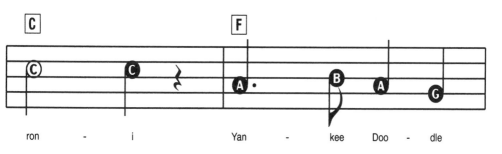

ron - i Yan - kee Doo - dle

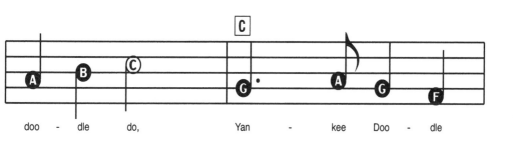

doo - dle do, Yan - kee Doo - dle

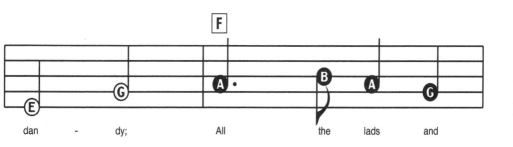

dan - dy; All the lads and

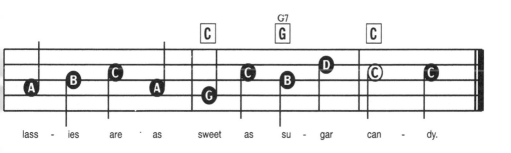

lass - ies are as sweet as su - gar can - dy.

You're a Grand Old Flag

Registration 2
Rhythm: Fox Trot

Words and Music by
George M. Cohan

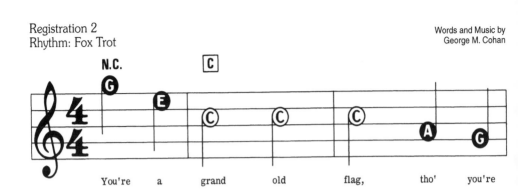

You're   a   grand   old   flag,   tho'   you're

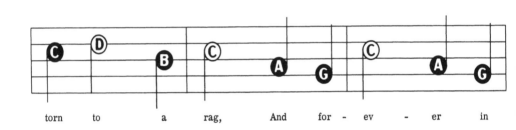

torn   to   a   rag,   And   for - ev - er   in

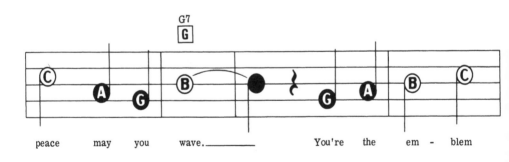

peace   may   you   wave._____   You're   the   em - blem

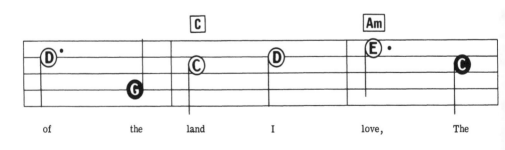

of   the   land   I   love,   The

Zacchaeus Was a Wee Little Man

Registration 8
Rhythm: Fox Trot

Traditional

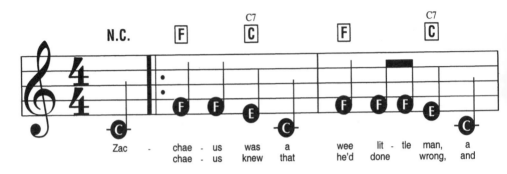

Zac - chae - us was a wee lit - tle man, a
chae - us knew that he'd done wrong, and

wee lit - tle man was he. He climbed up in a
sor - ry for his sins was he. "Lord, to the poor I'll

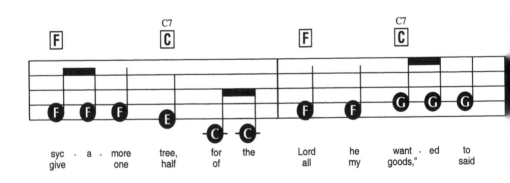

syc - a - more tree, for the Lord he want - ed to
give one half of all my goods," said

167

Registration Guide

- Match the Registration number on the song to the corresponding numbered category below. Select and activate an instrumental sound available on your instrument.

- Choose an automatic rhythm appropriate to the mood and style of the song. (Consult your Owner's Guide for proper operation of automatic rhythm features.)

- Adjust the tempo and volume controls to comfortable settings.

Registration

1	Mellow	Flutes, Clarinet, Oboe, Flugel Horn, Trombone, French Horn, Organ Flutes
2	Ensemble	Brass Section, Sax Section, Wind Ensemble, Full Organ, Theater Organ
3	Strings	Violin, Viola, Cello, Fiddle, String Ensemble, Pizzicato, Organ Strings
4	Guitars	Acoustic/Electric Guitars, Banjo, Mandolin, Dulcimer, Ukulele, Hawaiian Guitar
5	Mallets	Vibraphone, Marimba, Xylophone, Steel Drums, Bells, Celesta, Chimes
6	Liturgical	Pipe Organ, Hand Bells, Vocal Ensemble, Choir, Organ Flutes
7	Bright	Saxophones, Trumpet, Mute Trumpet, Synth Leads, Jazz/Gospel Organs
8	Piano	Piano, Electric Piano, Honky Tonk Piano, Harpsichord, Clavi
9	Novelty	Melodic Percussion, Wah Trumpet, Synth, Whistle, Kazoo, Perc. Organ
10	Bellows	Accordion, French Accordion, Mussette, Harmonica, Pump Organ, Bagpipes